Sabrina Mahfouz
Plays: 1

That Boy; Dry Ice; Clean; Chef; Battleface; the love i feel is red; With a Little Bit of Luck; Layla's Room; Rashida; The Power of Plumbing; This is How it Was

Sabrina Mahfouz has recently been elected a Fellow of the Royal Society of Literature and is the recipient of the 2018 King's Alumni Arts & Culture Award. She has won a Sky Arts Academy Award for Poetry, a Westminster Prize for New Playwrights and a Fringe First Award for her play *Chef*. Her play *With a Little Bit of Luck* won the 2019 Best Drama Production at the BBC Radio & Music Awards. She also writes for children and her play *Zeraffa Giraffa* won a 2018 Off West End Award.

Sabrina is the editor of *The Things I Would Tell You: British Muslim Women Write*, a 2017 Guardian Book of the Year, and the forthcoming *Smashing It: Working Class Artists on Life, Art and Making It Happen*. She is an essay contributor to the multi-award-winning *The Good Immigrant* and is currently writing a biopic of the rapper and producer Wiley, for Pulse Films.

Sabrina Mahfouz

Plays: 1

That Boy

Dry Ice

Clean

Chef

Battleface

the love i feel is red

With a Little Bit of Luck

Layla's Room

Rashida

The Power of Plumbing

This is How it Was

With an introduction by the author

methuen | drama

LONDON • NEW YORK • OXFORD • NEW DELHI • SYDNEY

METHUEN DRAMA
Bloomsbury Publishing Plc
50 Bedford Square, London, WC1B 3DP, UK
1385 Broadway, New York, NY 10018, USA

BLOOMSBURY, METHUEN DRAMA and the Methuen Drama logo are
trademarks of Bloomsbury Publishing Plc

This collection first published in Great Britain 2019
That Boy first published in this collection by Methuen Drama, 2019
Copyright © Sabrina Mahfouz, 2019
Dry Ice first published by Methuen Drama in *The Clean Collection*, 2014
Copyright © Sabrina Mahfouz, 2014
Clean first published by Methuen Drama in *The Clean Collection*, 2014
Copyright © Sabrina Mahfouz, 2014
Chef first published by Methuen Drama, 2015
Copyright © Sabrina Mahfouz, 2015
Battleface first published in this collection by Methuen Drama, 2019
Copyright © Sabrina Mahfouz, 2019
the love i feel is red first published in this collection by Methuen Drama, 2019
Copyright © Sabrina Mahfouz, 2019
With a Little Bit of Luck first published by Methuen Drama, 2016
Copyright © Sabrina Mahfouz, 2016
Layla's Room first published by Methuen Drama, 2016
Copyright © Sabrina Mahfouz, 2016
Rashida; first published in this collection by Methuen Drama, 2019
Copyright © Sabrina Mahfouz, 2019
The Power of Plumbing first published in this collection by Methuen Drama, 2019
Copyright © Sabrina Mahfouz, 2019
This is How it Was first published in this collection by Methuen Drama, 2019
Copyright © Sabrina Mahfouz, 2019
Sabrina Mahfouz has asserted her right under the Copyright,
Designs and Patents Act, 1988, to be identified as author of this work.
Cover image © WITCH Projects

A catalogue record for this book is available from the British Library.

A catalog record for this book is available from the Library of Congress.

ISBN: PB: 978-1-3501-4355-5
ePDF: 978-1-3501-4356-2
eBook: 978-1-3501-4357-9

Series: Contemporary Dramatists

Typeset by Mark Heslington Ltd, Scarborough, North Yorkshire

To find out more about our authors and books visit
www.bloomsbury.com and sign up for our newsletters.

Contents

Introduction

I had always been searching for a job which could give me a sense of power over my physical and mental self, as well as pay the bills. Strip clubs were the first places that provided some of that, however relative and youthfully misguided it may (or may not – I am still confused) have been, it was a place of feeling powerful within a single space for a finite time after navigating wilfully oppressive and violent societies for the entirety of my life to that point. Working within senior government was another attempt, Mayfair nightclubs another and, finally, the world of intelligence the last one before discovering writing.

'Discover' is a misleading term, as of course I had always written – or at least told stories. Before I could write, I recorded them on the tape player, sellotape over the cassette, to play back to myself and my long-suffering family. I'd studied literature all of my life, but I had never considered it something to do as a job; it was too enjoyable and I'd grown up seeing people regard jobs as purely a means to an end, not something they loved, so the two things did not join up for me. Even if it had, those platforms writing required and provided were not ones I felt I could ever stand upon. I didn't actually know that much about how varied these platforms could be until, one evening, I met a friend for a drink at the Southbank Centre when I heard a voice not too dissimilar to mine, a young woman's South London working-class accent with a performative edge to it, telling a surreal story into a microphone. It was Laura Dockrill, performing poems at a free event space at the centre, and I was mesmerised and galvanised. All the poems I had written and kept hidden at home came out of my mouth now; I did every open mic night going and kept attending and reading out loud in pubs and clubs and basements until I made the discovery that writing characters and bringing them to life on stage in a performance (which was quite different to acting, which I had also attempted at a much earlier stage) was what finally gave me that sense of power over aspects of myself that, in all other endeavours, at some point felt wrangled from my control. To take to a stage and have an audience listen to you, absorb your own words or however you are telling a story, is such a huge, magnificent privilege. It comes with difficulties, of course – paralysing insecurities, financial chaos, external and internal pressures of expectations and responsibilities to those you want to represent or centre etc. – but it remains, for me, the ultimate in empowerment for the context in which we are living right now. So my first performance pieces were short, character and poetry-based in that they had an internal rhyme and rhythm that dialled up to surrealism at times. I would always perform them myself. After enough people had asked why I didn't write for theatre (for the theatre that they thought of as theatre, i.e. writing dialogue-based plays for actors to act), I decided to give it a go and joined the Royal Court 'Unheard Voices' Writers Group for British Muslims. They don't do such identity-based groups anymore which is theoretically a good thing, as times *should* have moved along enough for all people to feel welcome and able to apply for these groups. Back then, I was certainly grateful to meet other writers who I felt such an immediate connection to and with whom I still work today, such as playwright and screenwriter Rachel De-lahay, poet and playwright Zia Ahmed, playwright, director and educator Shireen Mula and filmmaker Rumi Begum. Emboldened by being with other 'others', I realised the power of a script whilst part of this program. I had studied Shakespeare, Ibsen, Euripides, Sophocles and Aristophanes as an English Literature and Classics undergraduate, but I'd never really delved into contemporary theatre and so I wasn't seeing it as a particularly vital artform in the way I was with performance poetry or music. As part of the program we got discounted or free tickets to see plays at the Royal Court. I'd never seen anything there before; my theatre trips had been a few musicals with Brownie groups as a kid, plays we put on at school or the occasional Christmas treat to the panto. *random* by debbie tucker green was premiering. And once again, just like that time in the Southbank Centre, I was floored, mesmerised, galvanised. Stories on stage with accents I knew, lives that I knew – but not told in the realist soap-opera way that working-class lives seemed to always be told, from my limited viewing and reading experience. Poetic, specific, lyrical language bringing forth the most devastating story with such complex simplicity. I wasn't sure I had the heart for conveying such devastation, but I finally felt the theatre space was one I'd really like to write for, knowing it didn't have to be confined to living room scenes or witty, subtext-heavy, kitchen-based dialogue (which I love reading and watching in hundreds of plays, it's just not what I love to write).

Expanding out from writing-performing for myself to writing for other people to act allowed me to experiment with styles and subjects, so there was another element of reclaiming power that came from pushing myself out from the area of writing in which I had become comfortable. Over the ten years since then, adding fiction, libretti and screenplays to the mediums in which I have experimented has really impacted what story I choose to tell and how.

The plays and performance pieces in this anthology have individual notes attached to them written by me, briefly explaining how and why they came about, which of course meant re-reading them all and attempting to cast my mind back to the time of their creation.

Reading back on my first ever piece for the stage, a ten-minute play called *That Boy* from 2010, I was initially shocked at my seemingly casual and constant mentioning or actioning of violence against women, as well as my centring of the man protagonist rather than the woman. But the shock wore off quickly. That violence – by men against women, by narrow society norms about masculinity against men, and by narrow gender norms against everyone – was absolutely the central reason for me writing the piece and I have only realised it almost a decade later. The threat of physical violence that women can feel every time they are 'chatted up' by men, the accepting, calm, unconfrontational way in which they have learnt, consciously or not, to deal with these scenarios in a way that feels safest is all there, in Taps and Selena's exchange. But in 2010, the discourse and language around this was nowhere near as public and accessible as it is now – I hadn't processed or even discussed these things with my friends in any depth at all. I was attempting to do it in my first ever script. But I also made Taps likeable, Selena passive and mostly agreeable. Why? I think it came partly from consuming so many playscripts, films and TV episodes that did the same thing, that told me the man's perspective was the one I would be able to write and understand better and the one the audience would relate to more – completely ridiculous and yet completely understandable. When I saw the play performed at Soho Theatre and realised this is what I had done and why, I vowed to always centre women and non-binary people and challenge myself to overwrite what I had consumed with what I *knew*. Things have of course improved slightly in the theatre and screen industries – but not as much as people might think. I am, at the time of writing, one of only thirteen women to have a Methuen Drama play collection, from a 128-strong overall catalogue. The National Theatre was heavily criticised for a 2019 season in which no women writers featured at all and the same scenario, though less publicised, happens at theatres across the country. In 2018, seventy women TV writers wrote an open letter questioning the lack of women employed to write big shows – such as ITV having only one drama out of nine that year written by a woman.

This is all to say, it is wonderful to see work by those historically marginalised by the creative industries being celebrated when it occurs, but that celebration should not create the false impression that things are 'fixed' – no matter how many would love to argue this is the case. Violence against women occurs in every one of the plays in this collection in different ways because, to me, we live in a world where it is impossible to represent a woman's life and not show the violence – whether physical, mental, emotional or spiritual – she is subjected to on a daily basis, particularly if gender identity is intersected with other marginalised aspects such as class, race, religion, disability or sexuality.

The omission and obstruction of women and other marginalised groups writing and documenting is a form of violence, so to write and document in spite of that omission and obstruction is a form of revolution and resistance, even in these supposedly 'diverse' times. If you ever feel doubtful of your 'right' to write or are waiting to be given permission or validation – please remember this and do it anyway! We need you.

That Boy

That Boy began as a response to a writing exercise at a free Soho Theatre workshop I attended in 2010, which prompted us to begin a piece with four overheard lines of conversation, but set them somewhere different and carry it on. I found this so useful as a starting point and enjoyed writing it so much I decided to enter it into the Westminster Prize for New Playwrights, which called for plays by unproduced writers of fifteen minutes or less. It came second place and was produced at Soho Theatre. Whilst I do try to encourage people to not feel that they need the validation of prizes and awards to keep writing, there's no denying it acted as a significant catalyst for me to continue exploring writing for the stage. I expand on why it was written in the way that it was in the introduction to this book, but suffice to say here that it is my only play that centres on a male protagonist!

*There is a young woman, **Selena**, sitting on a tube carriage reading her book. She is dressed for a party; she has a large handbag with wine sticking out.*

*A young man, **Taps**, in a baseball cap and jeans sits opposite her. He is listening to his iPod and nodding to the tune. He is also staring intently at her and fidgeting, sitting low down on the seat. She is pretending not to notice and continues reading, even though they are almost alone in the carriage.*

Eventually, he leans forward and starts to speak to her, taking his headphones out. She looks cautiously up from her book but does not give him her full attention at first, but his good looks have caught her attention.

Taps   You look nice ya know.

Selena   Thanks.

Taps   Where you going?

Selena   My mate's birthday.

She looks at her phone.

I'm late you know.

Pause.

Taps   So, you single and that yeh?

Selena   Errr, yeah.

Taps *smiles and nods.*

Taps   That's good.

Selena   How old are you?

Taps   Nineteen. I look younger?

Selena   I guess. A bit.

Taps   Yeh girls tell me I got a baby face or summin, I ain't having that though, I look mature. Like Tupac don't you think?

Selena   That means you're so mature you dead. Not a good look.

Taps   Easy, respect for my man the king of rap.

Selena   Do you really reckon he's the king of rap? You musta been, like, five when he died or something.

Taps   So what, man can still appreciate the greats. The classics. And anyway you know I see this mad YouTube video taken last month in some dark up cave in Afghanistan or summin and I swear Tupac was in there. He ain't dead, no way.

Selena   What, he was freestyling with bin Laden?

Taps   True stories, this shit is deep.

Selena   What you listening to?

Taps   Nuttin. I got all the music I need looking at you.

Selena   What do you usually listen to then?

Taps   Depends on my mood.

Selena   What mood are you in now?

Taps   I'm happy, you know. (*He offers her one of his headphones.*) You want one?

Selena   Yeh, alright then.

He gets up and moves next to her so they can listen to the tune. They nod.

She is looking at his iPod.

Selena   It's well nice.

Taps   It's got a Dictaphone.

Selena   You been recording me?

Taps   Nah. I use it though sometimes.

Selena   You sing?

Taps Nah, that ain't me. I just, y'know, record my thoughts sometimes.

Selena Like a diary?

Taps Kinda. Yeh, kinda. I never been one for pen to page so yeh. I wanna know how I was feeling last month I just go into my folder on here, 'True Stories', and, yeh, have a listen innit.

Selena I'm more of a writer, but it's a good idea though. 'True Stories', you should think of a more original name, maybe you can make a book out of it when you're older.

Taps (*laughs*)   Man ain't gonna be no book writer, babes. How old are you?

Selena How old do you think I am?

Taps One of them ones yeh? Umm, bout twenty-two?

Selena What?! Do I really look that old?

Taps You don't look old, you look like a woman. A real woman. You look sophisticated. Like you know what you like, you know what you're about. You talk like a big woman too, I like it. That's what I'm looking for ya get me.

Selena Thanks, I guess.

Taps Where you going for your mate's birthday?

Selena Brixton.

Taps Seen. I'm from them sides, still.

Selena Is it?

Taps Yeh. Where you from?

Selena Walthamstow.

Taps That's far, man.

Selena Far from what?

Taps Briccy. Everyting.

Selena   Not really, only fifteen stops.

Taps   Ha you been counting dem yeh? Good job man got on when he did, rescue you an all that.

Selena   I was reading my book. I was alright.

Taps   You look more than alright you know.

Selena   Thanks.

Taps   Walthamstow yeah? That's not too far from where I been.

Selena   Where you been?

Taps   Barnsbury.

Selena   Why?

Taps   Been Pentonville innit.

Selena   Wha – why?

Taps   Nah nah I ain't an inmate don't worry bout that. Went to see my mate. He got time, man. He got time.

Selena   How long?

Taps   Fifteen years you know. Dude's only my age. He'll do half that with good behaviour, maybe out on tag in five or six, but still, it's a stretch.

Selena   Shit, what'd he do?

Taps   It's a long story, babe. What's your name?

Selena   (*holds up her book*)   I like stories. Selena. Tell me.

Taps   Alright then, pass the time I spose. My name's Taps by the way.

Selena   Taps?

Taps   Yeh, like those things in the bath you get water out of. Run hot and cold quick time.

Selena   Lets anyone turn them on?

Taps   Cheeky, I like it.

Selena   So, Taps, tell me the story.

Taps   It ain't pretty. And you a pretty lady, so I got to be sure you wanna hear it.

Selena   You said yourself, I'm a big girl.

Taps   Quick too. Shit, you're my perfect woman.

Alright, so check it.

My boy Shorts, that's who I just been to see. We grew up together – school, spitting, shotting, graffing – all that.

He used to come to my yard for breakfast early times cos his mum was always out. Sometimes she dint even come home at night. So he'd come to mine and my mumsy would feed him whatever we had, look after him like he was my brother. Shit, boy was my brother. Didn't never have another.

Me and Shorts, yeh, we were always inna tings, but small time. Shot some green here and there, sell a few Xboxes come Christmas an that, but never any big tings. We wanted to start a record label, go legit. Big dreamers, my mum used to say.

Anyway, he starts rolling with these man dem that I don't want nuttin to do with and we drift apart. He says he doing it all cos he don't wanna be known as just 'that boy from the ends', he wants to be the man. He wants everyone to know 'yeh that's Shorts'. You know how it is, Sel?

Selena   Yeah.

Taps   Then one day I hear from some gal I be banging at the time – sorry, but she was just any bang – she tells me that Shorts has been stabbed. In the head. In the fucking head. I was going mad, dint have a clue what to do, mash-up situation, ya get me. I'm powerless like that but I wanna help him.

Go see him at hospital – miracle the boy dun survive. He's alright, he's gonna live, he's a soldier, it's a miracle – that's what everyone kept saying.

But he weren't alright. From that day, my man was strange. Psychologically damaged, my mum said. This time here he just sat and stared. At the wall, the TV, his zute – whatever, just staring into space like he lost.

Selena   For real?

Taps   He got mad angry at things, stupid things like on *EastEnders* or some shit, and he'd hold his head and do some mad moaning noise. See him one time trying to strangle a cat on road. Doctors put him on some meds. He had more pills to take than a shotter in a rave, truss me.

Selena   That's so sad.

Taps   We thought he was alright. Started catching jokes with us again, staying away from the other crew. But then, one night, I get a call from the police station. They got Shorts. He ain't coming back.

Selena   Why? What happen?

Taps   He'd been visiting one of his old boys in prison. He was feeling vexed, the boy had took the wrap for him for some deal gone wrong time ago. Shorts felt bad, since it happen this boy had a baby and all sorts – long tings. Anyway, he gets the bus back home and sees a pretty girl, starts trying to chirps her. She weren't having none of it. She was like, 'You ain't that boy for me'. He'd been speeching her for ten minutes and so now he's like, 'What did you say? I ain't "that boy" for you? You sure as fuck I ain't "that boy" for no one. I'm Shorts and you best remember that.' She starts laughing at him, turns back round to read her book and he just stands up, grabs her by the hair and starts bashing her head against the bus window, raggo just like in daylight an everything.

By the time somebody stopped him, she'd stopped screaming.

Selena   Oh my God.

Taps   The window was dented, cracked – and you know them windows there ain't no joke ting. Her head was the same. She went to hospital and got sent home with brain damage. He got took off to the cells with blood on his hands and ain't been out since.

Selena   That is fucked-up. He shoulda got longer. Life. That poor girl.

Taps   I know man, it's a fucking tragedy. But then check this, they found out he hadn't taken his meds for the last week. But still, it wasn't enough for diminished responsibility.

Selena   Good.

Taps   What d'ya mean good? At least then he'd be in some nut house and getting some kinda help. Instead, he gonna come out in a few years even more fucked-up than when he went in. It ain't easy in there, y'know.

Selena   Yeh? And how easy is it gonna be for that girl? How much help can they give her brain after he bashed it to pieces on a fucking bus?! That boy deserves everything he gets. I hope he drops the soap in them showers every day.

Taps (*shouting and suddenly enraged*)   Fuck you talking bout? You don't understand this shit. And he ain't 'that boy', he's got a name yeh.

Selena   Alright.

Pause.

Taps   Sorry. It's been a hard day. I told you it weren't a pretty story. I'm sorry if I ruined your night.

Selena   Nah, you didn't.

Pause.

But boy, you must be a good friend, cos I don't know if I could go see my girl if she did summin like that, no matter how tight we'd been.

Taps   You can surprise yourself with what you capable of sometimes, babes.

Pause. Smiles.

Did I scare you just then? You look mad sexy when you scared.

Selena   You don't scare me. Anyway, do what you're doing, but watch out when he gets out that he's cool.

Taps   You worried for me?

Selena   Nah. You can look after yourself.

Taps   That I can. But I could look after you as well, Sel. And rhyme whilst I'm doing it. Big like that.

Selena   You joker.

Taps   You can call me whatever you want to babygirl, if you do one little thing for me.

Selena   Oh really, what's that then?

Taps   Come link me tomorrow?

Selena   I dunno . . .

Taps   Why not?

Selena   It's my mate's birthday innit. We doing girl things tomorrow.

Taps   Yeh, so? You ain't got a man. You do your thing then come link me and we can chill for a bit innit. I can do an Usher on you and play you my confessions.

Selena   Usher is butters, man. And chill? Ain't you even gonna offer me a nice meal or summin?

Taps   I ain't got funds for that right now, princess, straight up. But what I have got are moves.

He gets up from his seat and starts slow grind dancing.

Selena   Oh no. What are you doing?! You are nuts!

Taps (*sings while slow dancing*)
Sexy Selena – ooh
It's almost midnight
And I've been dying to kiss you
Under the tube light . . .

Selena (*laughing*)   Oh my God! Stop it!

Taps (*sings and dances*)
Sexy Selena
There's no need to run away
Girl, I'm begging you please won't you stay

He is kneeling down and she is laughing, shaking her head.

Selena   Aren't you shamed yet?!

Taps (*gets up, sings and dances*)
I've only just met ya
Feels though I've known you for a lifetime
Tell me do you feel like I do
I really wanna get ya –
You came along at just the right time
I get a blue sensation with you.

He finally coerces her to get up and they dance together while he sings and she looks around, embarrassed but loving it.

Sexy Selena – ooh
It's almost midnight
And I've been dying to kiss you
Under the tube light.
Sexy Selena
There's no need to run away
Girl, I'm begging you please won't you stay –

He is reaching a big crescendo and she joins in:

I'm begging you pleeeease won't yooooooou –

She looks out of the carriage window. The tube has stopped at a station. They've passed some young men at the other end of the platform who peered in as best they could when they passed and now their distant shouts can be heard:

Young Men (*offstage*)   I swear it's that boy! . . . Yes, bruv, I'm telling you it is, it's him! . . . That boy's gonna get it . . .

Selena   Do they know you, Taps?

Taps   Nah. But I don't wanna cause any trouble for you.

The doors open, running is heard.

I'm gonna bounce. You have a good party though yeh? Enjoy yourself. Take time, babes. And take this.

He holds out his iPod with the headphones dangling.

Selena   But why – wha –

Taps   You like it, innit?

She nods.

So keep it yeh, for me?

She looks at it, stares at him. He puts it in her hand. She shrugs.

Selena   Alright. Thanks.

Taps   Don't thank me. True Stories, babes.

He runs off the tube as the doors close and he turns to wave before running out of the station.

Selena (*under her breath*)   True Stories.

She sits down and puts the headphones in her ears. She counts the stops to go and carries on reading her book.

Dry Ice

Dry Ice was many years in the making – in my head, on till receipts, order pads and that old cliché, napkins. I scribbled things as I worked in strip clubs, during quiet moments, on the way home, in the toilets, in the bar stockroom. It began with a series of poems that I would perform as part of my poetry sets and by 2011, with the encouragement of people in poetry and theatre such as Natalie Ibu, Mike Bartlett, Francesca Beard, Ola Animishawun and Salena Godden, I wanted to put these poems together in some kind of theatrical narrative – Nina and *Dry Ice* is what came out. I developed some ideas with High Tide's Genesis Lab and produced a scratch of it at New Wimbledon Theatre at the Studio, followed by a debut run at Edinburgh Fringe Festival, by which time David Schwimmer came on board as director and helped the show reach a wider audience, including the artistic director of the Bush Theatre at the time, Madani Younis, who programmed it to play in a double bill with Caroline Horton's *You're Not Like The Other Girls Chrissy* in 2012 and was the start of a continuing artistic partnership and friendship. It was the play that was bursting my heart to come out and it was the one that gave me the opportunity to create many others. It will always maintain such a special place for me because of this context.

The heavy stage directions at the start were specific to the (extremely low-budget) production I was performing in and producing – they were notes for me and my team, so I wouldn't want anyone to feel they are essential to the show at all, if thinking of using the text to perform.

Dry Ice was first performed in Edinburgh on 4 August 2011 at the Underbelly Cowgate as part of the Edinburgh Fringe Festival with the following cast and creative team:

Nina   Sabrina Mahfouz

Director   David Schwimmer
Producer   Sabrina Mahfouz
Assistant Director/Producer   Riz Ahmed
Costume Designer   Molly Rowe
Costume Assistant   Hannah Hopkins
Composer   Anne Chmelewsky

Characters

Nina plays all characters and is any ethnicity, North England accent

Notes on the text:
Sections in quote marks and normal font = a character is speaking to another character

No quote marks and normal font = character narrating to audience

Quote marks and italics = Nina playing another character within her own character

Empty stage save for a chair centre stage. Pre-show music and pre-show lights up. House lights fade. Pre-show music and lights fade, leaving a pool of light on stage around the chair and . . . silence.

Nina *enters with an oversized bag containing all her costumes, props and lights. She stops upstage centre, takes a look at the audience and smiles.*

She puts the bag down and first takes out a long string of lights, plugging them in (but they do not go on) and creating a large circle around the chair.

She removes various objects from the bag, setting the stage.

She puts on her protective gloves and goggles – but leaves them on her forehead for now.

She moves to her start place, downstage of the chair, and nods to the lighting operator – puts goggles over eyes, which cues lights to black and, at the same time, circle of lights come on.

Lights up as she does a sequence of three 'model' poses and –

Scene One: The First Night

Nina I'm standing in my being-renovated bathroom, trying on these bits and bobs of 'health and safety equipment' the builders have left. Ma boyfriend, P, leans on the wall having a beer, watching me.

P 'What are ya doing?'

Nina 'What's it look like?'

P 'Err, like you've lost the fucking plot, love.
Serious babe, what are you doing?'

Nina He asks again and I pity his little brain as I explain very clearly:

'I'm assessing Personal Protection Equipment.

There's quite a selection here, actually. The builders left it. (*Reading.*) "To allow the right type of PPE, Personal Protection Equipment, to be chosen for you, carefully consider the hazards of the workplace." Geddit? My workplace?'

His face, blank. His eyes not seeing how PPE could relate to me but enjoying the sight of his woman in a boiler suit, nevertheless.

P   'Riiiight. Well come on, nutcase, get dressed. We'll be late for dinner.'

Nina   There's two hours to go. And he always takes the most amount of time anyway. I think, piss off, but instead:

'Sweetheart, can you adjust these goggles please?

They're so tight I can hardly see.

Thanks.

The reason I need these, it says here, is to provide protection from radiation, metal files, dust – ahaa, projectiles!

Quite fitting, don't you think?

So that when those winking weirdos in the front row get a little hand-happy, I can slap my leg around the pole, back bend down low and not worry about having to wipe any . . . thing out of my eye.

I feel safer already.'

Now he's got a steady gaze, eyes locked onto me cos he can feel it getting interesting.

Dirty details, that's what he likes. So I oblige.

'The hard hat, babe, pass it. Do you think I could wear it on the side? Oi, oi mister, in for a rough ride?! Ha.

This one, says here, is suitable for protection from "falling objects"; "head bumping" – oh baby I can hear your heart proper thumping there.

Ah, "hair entanglement". That's more like it, although hair entanglement can often be a plus – move a sec please, P, I'm just going to demonstrate how, help me out. Come on then, say something.'

Nina *gets into 'stripper-mode' and pulls chair in front of her, pretending a client (or* **P***) is sitting on it.*

P   'Ere darlin', I ain't seen a body that tight in a while.'

Nina   'Really? Thanks.

A crooked tooth through an angel smile.

The teasing tassels get caught in the red velvet chair, she distracts him by thrashing her *entangled* hair in his face he got a taste, he likes it doesn't he?

So he should he's not getting this for free.'

P   'How much?

What? I didn't even get to touch. This has got to be a joke, some Eastern Bloc chick would at least let me have a poke for that kind of cash. I mean I might look flash, but I'm jus an ordinary bloke who likes to do a bitta coke, ave a laugh – I deserve it after all me hard graft.

Missus might not agree but then she ain't here to see so who gives a shit.

Fuck it, tell me how you'd like to suck it.

Yeh, yeh I'll give you my card charge what you want just keep me this hard.'

Nina   'Ah you do make me laugh, P.'

She laughs. Picks up and puts on a respirator from the things the builders left.

Nina   I put this on my nose and he snaps out of his hard-faced horny pose rising up from the chair with a –

P   'Respirator? Oh drop me out Nina.

How do you reckon that one's gonna help ya then?'

Nina   I remain zen-like as I say without a trace of irony: 'Don't you know the smells men emit when they're trying to get a piece, babe?

There's the nasty fumes from the too-spicy pre-strip post-show dinner they had – oh and then the stink from the aftershave kept in the toilets next to the marble sink by the attendant – pop a pound in his hand and it's all yours for three sprays.

They come back and I never stay then – fucking reeks, can't breathe let alone speak. Yuck.'

P   'True say. I know . . . my boys do that when they're on the pull.

Anyway, babe, come on, we're gonna be late.

Oh yeh, and your mum's coming to stay.'

Nina   He drops it like it's nothing. Like it's something I hear everyday.

Says it like I want to hear it.

'What? When?'

P   'Tomorrow.'

Nina   'For how long?'

P   'Dunno, she didn't say. What's wrong, it's not that bad, is it?'

Nina   'No I guess not.'

The accusing look on his face reminds me of the house mum at work fining me for getting to the pole late or for having a superhero outfit on when it was St Trinian's night.

I mean, right or wrong, I'd never told my mum that I was going to become a stripper.

I just didn't think it was a career that would hit her as something to tell the neighbours about, no matter how much they loved Nicole from the Pussycat Dolls.

Oh, if I had of told her, then the accusing look on her face would have been a thousand times worse than P's had just been.

Actually, this vision, of my mum's God-fearing, accusing face, was pretty much all I could see when I made it to the club for my first night of 'exotic dancing'.

(Although I learnt early on that dancing is the smallest part of the show and the money's where your fingers go.)

On that first night I was so scared. I had fun though and pretty much met all the types I would meet over the next four years.

Lemme tell ya about them.

So. Number one and most abundant are 'The Regular Lads' Lads', most of whom proudly announce themselves as dads and have photos of their little, sweet Maisie in their wallets which they flash shamelessly as they take out their Visa Debit to pay for your last naked, wet twenty minutes.

They're there with their friends, they'll claim.

'Our wives know it's the thing to do on a night out – Christ, they got into the trend of pole-dancing classes down the gym so they can't exactly whip our arses for enjoying the expertise of a proper striptease, can they darlin'?'

Course not, no.

'But bloody hell, it is a shame about the price. Any chance of a two for one ahaha.'

Knobs. And worth avoiding at most costs.

Number two type.

The number two type was, due to my judgemental stereotyping mind, the one I was already most familiar with – but of course he really does exist.

Sweat in beads at the back of a fat neck peering jeerily out of a starched white shirt which alerts everyone but the wearer to the jut-out belly like a cut-out copy of a cartoon family guy.

Mouth open with grunts and pleadings for you to *'lean in a bit closer sweet thing, yeh, wag those fun bags right here'* as his tongue licks slippy lips you can avoid his puffed-lid eyes by staring into the inside of his smoky black mouth, like the inside of a burnt-out building that's been flash backed, glowing cinders now fat with hardened ash which the squatter smoking blowbacks scrapes aside.

The kind of type to make you question how much you really want to continue this life as he rifles through pinstriped pockets, writes his number on a dry-cleaning docket and reckons you're friends now cos when you bent over and he touched your thigh you didn't tell security to do him in so now he grins and tells you
'You're a good girl int ya, a naughty good girl'.

Curls his finger round the score you charge and ignores the fact that you're retching like a car engine at the very sight of him.

Although to be fair, depending how much I've been drinking, I sometimes think 'ah poor thing'.

But that's only til he brings his clientele over, says that you'll bowl them over and probably let them get hand happy if they tip you an extra ten. Ten! Then raises eyebrows at you secretly, like he's just struck you a deal Ronaldinho or someone would be happy with. Prick.

The third type: The In-Betweeners.

The squeamish, *'oh-I-don't-really-wanna-be-here'*-rs.

The – *'I don't know, I've got a great girl at home ones'* – who try to relax by preferring to *'just have a chat'* and ask about your life story like it's as interesting as the ten girls who've gone before and then, just as your five minutes no-dancing time (breach of which incurs a fifty quid fine) is up, he drops his business card on the floor.

Says *'You should call me, I'd, er, really like to know more – if you give me your number I'll definitely think about buying a dance a little later on, when I've, y'know, had a bit longer to feel more . . . comfortable.'*

Take the card, fake a smile, a past number left and a very real 'fuck you, mate', said under your breath.

Now, the fourth and final type.

This is the secretive, filthy rich, tailored suit executive, the lucrative customer, the one all the girls crave will save them from this doldrums life of doll dressing up and whisk them off to St Tropez to stay in his mansion.

Or at least buy them a Gucci bag.

Sometimes he does. Sometimes he doesn't.

That's how he maintains his buzz – unpredictability, mystery.

The bulge in his pocket – wads of fifties or evidence of over-average virility? Who can say? Except for the girl he chooses for his sit-down. His hour of private whore. Of private dance and private talk.

Of wanting more but not getting it, cos that's what he came here – and not a brothel – for, he reminds her, after she asks him if he wants *'extra service later on'*.

'Don't get me wrong,' he'll smoothly say, *'I find you terribly attractive, I just like to give.'*

Winks, sinks a few red notes into the rubber-grip top of nail-nicked stockings and sits back, never mistaken, never taken for a ride or a fool, never found drooling onto suit lapels or incapable of making his own way up the stairs.

Likes to appear to care, just enough to make us appear to care back. Lacks patronising tones, has enough phone numbers to give you one which won't get him into trouble and lives in a world so far removed from the real one that you actually, for that hour, make a perfect couple in a perfect bubble.

In each of these type-groups, there's always one.

Usually the young, never tongue tied always in a tie guy who feels the guilt all deep suddenly cos he's just spilt half his future kids all over the blue velvet seat so they try to ask questions like: *'How did you get into this? What are your dreams, your goals? When are you going to leave this place?'*

Turns to face you, eye to eye for the first time –

'What does your mother think?'

My first night, the first dance I ever did *that's* what I got congratulated with: *'What does your mother think?'* About what, about the fact that I just gyrated my bare arse in time to 'Girls, Girls, Girls' in front of your face as you unfurled your wrap and sniffed a line off my thigh?

Dunno, why don't you ask her?

What does *your* mother think?

On your first night, right, you can't think.

You'll sink. You just dance, count, prance, mount.

Flirt, curt, doesn't hurt.

Up, down, around and around.

Head back, back arched, down the wine, throat's parched.

Spin, sin, enter the PIN, throw your dirty knickers in the bin, scrub skin, rub it in, can't sleep, adrenalin –

'P, who's your heroine?'

P   'Err, I dunno. Ain't ya mum, that's for sure.

Get ready and you might be, for tonight, anyway.'

They kiss. Lights off. Music.

Scene Two: The Dinner

Nina   At the neighbours now. Well, a few roads away anyway.

Reminds me what a fancy part of town this is.

Family photos of snow mountains criss-crossed with ski scars, like a gangster's cheek well-healed, sit poised in picture frames perched on the fireplace and when no one is looking I aim my trigger finger – pow! – at the one with the twins doing snowboard spins with their helmets on.

P is looking shaky, hands through hair every second and a second cigarette between his lips.

P   'Would you like to go there one day, babe?'

Nina   'Wipe your nose, P, for God's sake.'

Lucinda   'It's nearly ready! Come on through, we've got some dirty martinis on the go, taking it back to the eighties, the golden age!'

Nina   P nods at Lucinda in agreement, wipes his nose –

P   'I'd say.'

Nina   The dining room's heating up.

The table's set, the Madagascan vanilla scented candles are lit.

The lights are off, we're all in our spots.

(*Pointing to positions as names are said.*) Larry, Susie, Dave, Lucinda, P and me.

I'm waiting to lick the last of my Grey Goose from the three queen green olives that are skewered on my martini stick, whilst P licks arse, pretends he knows about art and everyone seems high as a kite so I'm worried I'll be the only one with an appetite and look like a right greedy bitch – but luckily they all stop chatting shit and get stuck into the braised beef and wet paprika polenta so I guess the buzz was alcohol only, for now.

The table bends in the middle with the weight of the New Wave Heal's plates and my head aches with the boredom of their art dealing; prescription drug comparing; wannabe grown-up conversation.

They're all just as bored as me it seems, as I'm soon recruited in to tell stories of my 'exotic' life of oiled-up limbs and two-grand tips.

I got loads of them, so I begin . . .

'If ever there was such a thing as a wholesome stripper – she was it.

She had huge tits, which wobbled like peach jelly when she walked and hips that could sink ships with one swift wave of a sashay.

But instead, she used them as a mother would, bringing us Earl Grey tea on a polished silver tray, and we'd sip it in the changing room from cups that were made of such fine white china that the wilder girls would sometimes try and grind them into lines.

She was so kind, the kind of woman who offered us smiles and mints when hearts were sinking with the weight of rejection, who affectionately rallied us to count the joys of our job as we sobbed, wishing we'd been born boys.

We were never sure how she made any money, she was always so busy treating us to teatime breaks and honeydrop cakes and fending off the fakes

(those are the twats that didn't want to pay)

until one day I peeped into the private room, the one where no one except the wholesome one was allowed to go.

Peeping through a hole as small as a small toenail
I spied puffed plush pillowed points of reference pointing in deference to the middle of the room.

And there, there were no poles.

Just a stripper shoe on the floor, high-rise plastic soles half-covered in sand, a seaweed-stained hand caressing a greenish scaly tail.

I was trying to understand what was the hell was going on.

I felt a swell sail up, rise in my tassle-covered tummy and turned my head down and around.

I'd never been fond of the seaside, the thick smell of the sea floor had always made me feel unclean and a scar of sand would land me in the shower with a loofer for hours.

And now the scent of picked up pebbles and webbed feet permeated through the very door I stood at, though I was on dry ground.

Looked up again, rigid, ready, I couldn't quite believe what I'd found.

I saw her face. Full of flirty smiles and crafty glances down to her sequin-tipped tail which flick-flicked into the top of the top clients' drinks.

They were sinking into their chairs with looks of unchecked desire, loosening their silk ties, pulling their trousers up from the knee a little higher.

The wholesome stripper, the motherly figure full of tea and sweets who was before me now without any feet, was nearly swimming in red-hued notes as they floated down to the ground having been poked in awe into her shell-covered bra.

All this time of wondering when and how she worked, rumours asserting they'd seen her get cash for going down on the Filipino busboy with the strangely shaped tash.

But at least now I knew the truth, she'd managed to get paid because she was really a mermaid.

And everyone's heard all about the fetishes men have with fish.

How they wish they could grab both fins, massage the moist slime slowly between their fingers, avoid beady eyes

(cos they're placed on the side of the head)

and just stare, uninterrupted, at the smooth, oiled-up body instead.

So it made perfect sense that she was wealthy, men so enjoy an oddity, a freak show.

One from below water was more than they could hope for – but back to the dark door of the private room through which I was peeping due to an unobstructed keyhole.'

I'm about to get embroiled in the belly of the tale, when Larry has to say, with his greasy, spiky hair –

Larry   'Be fair now, Nina, you don't take us for complete fools, do you?'

Nina   Silence as I survey the turned-down eyes of the guilty other five.

A race to the water jug. Glug. Glug. Glug.

I take a generous slug of 1990 Krug.

'Fools, no. Bores, perhaps. Voyeurs, definitely. Pervs – well, you tell me.'

P *raps his napkin-covered knuckles on the table –*

P   'There weren't really no need for that, was there, babe?'

Nina   'I just gave an honest answer, no harm done, isn't that right, Dave?'

Dave nods and smiles, his reddened lips licking the words right out of my mouth.

Dave   'Not at all. In fact, it is an *absolute pleasure* to have such an *entertaining* young lady dining with us for a change.

Do continue to court us with your *extraordinary* tales Nina, I'm *intrigued*.'

Nina   Susie tries to make things right by asking me:

Susie   'Do you ski, Nina?'

Nina   'No, I don't like to do anything that involves wearing too many clothes.'

Lucinda gets up, red from the tip of her nose down, and makes a silently disgusted sound as she runs back round to the kitchen to take care of dessert.

Dave continues to flirt shamelessly but he's looking at P a bit funnily so I wonder if it's really me he fancies?

Larry frowns good-naturedly, eyes wide under bushy brows –

Larry   'Well, go on then. Bores need to be entertained, don't they?

Another story?'

Nina   'Well, couldn't hurt I spose.'

P breathes a sigh of relief. His authenticity about to be restored. He's got a wannabe Banksy in the back of the car and he's hoping they'll wanna buy it after the after-dinner cigar. I play my part to provide entertainment fitting for the girlfriend of an up and coming art part drug dealer who's rumoured to always have his eye on the next big thing. Little does he know they're much more interested in what he provides for the nose than the eyes. But I can't deal with him when he cries, so I start my story:

'Lucy loved to make lists.

Lists, lists, lists about how many times that week she'd got pissed and what she'd drank when she did.

Lists about the fibs she'd told the blokes who didn't want to know how old you really were, if you got a 2:1 in early Byzantine history and on your nights off you and your mum just got a Chinese.

These lists were phenomenal.

They papered her bedroom walls like vertical bricks and showed no sign of slowing down even when her family left town and she had to rent a storage space in which to place these undigitalised surprises of human strangeness.

Unlike others, she took notes at work rather than coke and as that was a far less stressful liability the managers ignored her paper habit and her regulars bit the end of her pen mid-dance thinking she was eccentrically writing sweet rhymes about them.

Little did they know they'd soon join lists about which ones tried to touch her tits, lists about which bits of some men she'd like to cut off with a blunt spoon, shallow fry and feed to her pet snake called Madam Doom.

Lists about which ones had wives, kids, picked their noses, scratched their balls, bought her roses, drove her up the wall; which liked cosy sit-downs or just wanted to crown her ample arse with cash.

Anyway, you get the idea.

So you can guess what an attractive aide she made when some psycho prick started slitting strippers' throats like he was waging a one-man war in a borderless world.

Night after night he skipped from club to club and in the small hours of every morning, a lonely lady would be found out back – throat slit, slumped like a derailed velvet curtain on the gravelled ground.

The boys in blue came in plain clothes.

Poked their fingers in our lockers, through our hair, stared at us in CCTV slow mo, traced our fortune from hands to wrists to – until at last they thought they'd struck gold with Lucy's lists.

She told me later she wished she'd burnt them, they became such a burden of truth which yet shed no light on the might-be identity of the serial killer who only had eyes for strippers.

I knew a few girls who fell to his blade.

Such a shame, such a waste of life.

They never found him.

In fact, he's still at large and they give us quarterly health and safety sessions on how to live in the shadow of a stripper throat slitteeeeeeer –

Lucinda   'Shiiiit!'

Nina   Lucinda shouts out –

Lucinda   'the brulee's bloody burnt!'

Nina   I turn to P and he looks at me lovingly, but then turns away and makes me feel that same way I do when he doesn't come home and the light in the photo frame reflects the TV and I think he's moving next to me.

The brulee is placed on the table and sure enough the rough brown sugar round the edges has turned black but the sticky top's still soft enough to crack so I give it a tap with the back of my silver spoon and when my mouth's full,

P realises it's high time to win them all around, so he says:

P   'Did Nina ever tell you about that girl from her work who went on *X Factor*?

You're sure to have heard of 'er – int they, babe?'

Nina 'Sure to have heard.'

Everyone 'Who? Who? Who? Who?'

Nina 'Beautiful, she was.

With skin that flinged back the light like the tip of a cliff licks the sky.

With illuminous dark hair that skimmed the air like it was about to make a shiny black waterfall full of follicles. Impossible, I know but anyway, it was her singing that took the world by storm.

Fan groups were formed on a minute by minute basis, pictures of her face were torn from magazines, downloads of her live performances were obscene – numbers so high whole towns were blocked, stopped from getting Wi-Fi so they rewound and crowned her princess of their SkyPlus – trust me, it was next level.

She'd never expected it. She was just a girl from an estate in Essex who loved her mum. And happened to work nights on a pole at the same club as me cos she chose to. The tabloids had more fun than if a footballer had shagged a royal, cos not only was she a stripper, she also had a long past full of gangs and drugs and convictions for muggings and grievous bodily harm. But she swore down she was calm now. The only thing she felt crazy about was winning – and singing of course. The public voted in their millions, her winning was such a sure thing bookies stopped taking bets. She'd come into work to vacate her locker, get her shoes and make-up bag and say goodbye. We hugged and cried and sang with fags in our hand. But then her ex-man had to intervene.

He'd not been too happy about her world domination, specially seeing as he required round the clock medical attention from where he'd taken a shot in the back on a job they'd done that had gone very wrong.

Bonnie and Clyde, Beyoncé and Jay-Z – that's what she used to tell him they could be. But that was before. Now he tore his hair from his head in fits of rage about the life she was living whilst he shat in a bag and got calloused hands from the two wheels that hardly concealed his immobility.

Despite his ailments he still had a few fail-safe street soldiers from back in the day that would keep food from their own kids for him, he would always be their king.

So on his orders, they kidnapped the now famous girl's mum and crossed barbed wire and borders to make sure they wouldn't be found.

The girl, my friend, was beside herself even when Cheryl Cole told her the judges' expense accounts were there for just this sort of thing (and Cheryl were actually quite excited, almost missing the criminality of her own upbringing).

The ransom wasn't money though, the demand was simple: she had to go. Leave the show. The world screamed out in a unanimous NO!

But she did it. She left and the mother was returned safely, but the poor girl was soon left bereft anyway as the dear mum couldn't stand the huge sacrifice her daughter had made, so her heart stirred and it started to break and one day she never woke up from the ache.

Sad, innit.

Crazy, but last I heard she was seen wheeling him around Westfield, in the village where all the posh shops are – Louis Vuitton I think it was, so I guess in the end it didn't all go that wrong.'

I stop and look around the table, there were tears in the eyes of the women but the men, who had hoped for something more saucy, had taken to doing lines with P as the tray was passed from seat to seat.

They'd still enjoyed it. Dave said:

Dave 'Well, Nina, that's simply a terrible story but you tell it terribly well!'

Nina Everyone laughs, except me cos it's so obviously not funny and clouds of white dust settle on the white tablecloth next to caramelised crumbs and become invisible.

P's still chuckling like a lick-arse when he says:

P 'When the tray's all done who's up for coming down to the car to have a look at the art I've got? It's top, it really is.

You're not gonna get many a chance to grab something like this.

Such straight art street art that's gonna be massive. Huge.

Queues of people already wanting it, but I knew I'd save it for you lot first, see what you thought.'

Nina A sea of nods. Larry, a city boy banker with stacks of cash and a yearly bonus the GDP of a small, insignificant country, pipes up, with coke still on the tip of his nose –

Larry 'I suppose you'll deny that street art has had its day then, P?

It's not just a convenient way for rich people to feel cool without having to leave their luxury behind?'

P 'Bollocks, Larry, the sun ain't even risen on its day yet.

That whole Banksy thing was just the start, just the call to all the real artists to get out there and show people what they got.

And they've got it, Larry, they have.

Kids with real talent.

Raw, undiluted, the law of the land disregarded and freedom, freedom personified in a spray can.

This shit's going to be moving for millions for the next century. Or more – why not? What's Van Gogh got that they ain't ay? Anger, passion, aloof, alone, outgrown the creative constricts of a society that don't recognise their genius – this is serious cultural commentary, people.

(*Coughs.*) Apparently.

Are you coming to see it or shall I bring it up?'

Susie   'Oh do bring it up, P, it sounds just, amazing.'

Nina   P's on a roll now, he can see they're eating out his hand now but it's getting rowdy and late and I try to pull him away whisper away tell him I've got so many bits to put away if my mum is coming to stay tomorrow.

Stockings, sequins, school-girl costumes.

And he knows I've got to be at work by twelve – that's just two hours away.

But he whispers for me to '*just go away*', he'll be fine on his own, so why don't I be a good girl and get a cab home.

So, stories done I walk, won't run, to the front door and I wait in between the Nicole Farhi furs for the Addison Lee to come and pick me up, take me home.

Scene Three: The Mum

At home.

Nina   My mum's dead religious. So religious she's not scared of death one bit. But shits herself at what the neighbours might say if any aspect of her life strays from the norm in any way. Mad that, isn't it? She'd have a straight-out heart attack if she knew about (*holds up a garter*) all this. She's not been to stay before, so I'm not really sure why she's chosen now. Maybe she's noticed how far apart we've grown the past couple of years. Maybe she's coming to check that I still know how to pray. Which I do.

I pray every night for a number four type that secretive,
lucrative, tailored suit executive to come in and make my
night worth the bunions and all the bloody bother.

But other than that . . . no, she'd be disappointed.

You know, sometimes I come home and I sit and I gaze and
I think about the days I've saved from beans on toast and
trips to the coast and a life made out of batter . . . then I look
in the mirror and I think – twenty-four, but you're so old.

And I go back to when I was young, to when time was
swallowed by my Swatch Watch.

When I threw plums on car windows with the boy from next
door, hidden by broken branches and Mum would come
storming out in her thick glasses, an umbrella in her hand to
look more serious and me and him'd piss ourselves laughing
– til we had to stay in for three days straight. I hated her
then.

Then came the time when she hated me, cos I was a
tearaway teen.

Mean to Mum in the most evil ways. Kray twin things but I
was all solo no brother or sister to soften the blow of your
only child turning into a wild, uncontollable bitch. I hit her
and I bit her and I told her she was a witch of a mother and
I'd have done anything to start my life again with another
one.

She used to scream her dreams at me, cos I'd been
promising til year ten when A-star grades laid on the top of
my ink-stained desk, every test passed though I spend every
class flicking magazines keen to cut out

'positions of the fortnight'

'how to be forthright in bed'

'how to give good head'

'ten-second sex tricks'

that'll make him stay with you, tell you, you're beautiful.

My head's full of equations persuading my maths teachers to make arrangements for my higher education earlier than most; Mum and neighbours toast to my success.

But I measure the size of my breasts against the picture, the poster, the film, the advert for cream sofas in soft leather I squeeze them together, wondering whether my cleavage is deep enough, my skin is smooth enough to put me on the pages of *FHM* – so I can blend blend blend in with the ideal of a real woman that is so real in my mind that I can't wait to find a man that will appreciate my ten-second sex tricks and pay for all my spray tans.

I dream of being on Page 3.

Of seeing my name in a bubble by my thighs *'Nina, 18, says she's dismayed by the current levels of obesity in Britain. She'd love to encourage a fitter, slimmer nation.'*

I didn't have to wait too long.

I'm eighteen years and five days and I'm amazed to find myself in a top city slick office with floor to ceiling glass and I laugh as they hand me a glass of champagne and tell me:

'Nina, we love your name, your look, your style, your smile, your dimples, your simple charm – you darling, are disarming. And although we'd love to keep you all to ourselves, up here, filed on our shelves, we just have to share you with the world.'

My lips curled so close to my eyes I thought I might die.

Was due on Page 3 in January.

I never knew Mum found the contract in December, but come the day of the shoot, she locked me in my room and wouldn't let me go. There were hundreds of girls waiting to fill my boots, so they never called me back. To pay her back I never went to university and now she thinks I work in sales. But I mean, I could still go to uni. And I'd likely sail through, cos now I know so much more than I knew.

Anyway, six years later and look at me. Sorta wealthy, still pretty, happy – and sometimes I think she wouldn't even be that upset if I told her. There's a lot of similarities between my mum's *religious* world and mine.

Like: kissing metal instead of flesh; testing patience, tolerance and common sense. Big booming male voices echoing demands and advice and promises of forgiveness and riches and redemption – except for some, who've just gone too far. Confessions of guilt that's given a one-way listen and hope, the hope of a new life, risen after this one.

So yeh, very similar – obviously mine's a lot more fun, but not sure Mum would see it like that.

She'd probably say it was a: (*Shouting.*) '*Dangerous, sinful, foul-living evil blow-job giving life of an ever damned never forgiven devil dancing dirty little godless whore!*'

Oh shit, I knew it, I'm late for work.

Lights off. Music.

Scene Four: The Work

Nina   Changing-room cheer.

The best part of the night, as long as there's no newbie Eastern Euros itching for a cat-fight to protect their pitch.

I file my nails and collect tales for mine and P's next dinner date. Existentialist conversationalist, Maria, is one of my favourites. Still here after eight years but with a never-ending stream of information about why you shouldn't be – reams of facts and figures about strippers who've never married, who've carried their secrets to the grave and not had a solitary tear shed at their funerals.

Anecdotes about coke-fiend friends whose noses have exploded on stage and they've been billed for the cleaning.

She always sits legs apart in cream lace, arched eyebrows so far apart her face seems to take up miles of space and she never shouts, smokes a lot. Her voice has got that gorgeous husk that's sent to those on twenty a day and she's posh. Not loads, but more than most of us here.

All the new girls fear her, say they see her as an evil stepmother type who doesn't like their youth and their nubile figures – but the reality is *they're* the ones who don't like the truth that threatens to burst out of her 1940s made-up mouth at any given second. It's like she's constantly checking round corners and peering over doors for the moment someone falls and then, bam, hits them with it. She just did it now.

One of the girls who started last month was acting all tough, shouting about how some new, tighter legislation over strip clubs was rubbish:

Aussie   'Can't they see there's not a thing wrong with what we do? I mean bloody hell, it's a free choice, it's a free country isn't it? I feel like stabbing them in the eye with my stiletto, get them to see.'

Nina   And Maria pipes up, from behind her feather boa –

Maria   'To see what, dear? How free we are?

You mean in here or, just . . . generally?'

Nina   A short sentence. Innocent sounding enough.

But there's something about Maria's rhetoric that gets stuck in your throat and doesn't let go. But Aussie let it go and went back on stage after her hair got sprayed.

Now old-timer Tanya puts down the straighteners, says to Maria:

Tanya   'Why have you got to be such a horrible bitch?'

Nina   Maria doesn't even flinch –

Maria 'Oh do shut up, Tanya, you're just put out because the word's got about that you got caught getting fingered in booth number two.

But I don't judge, we do what we have to do when you get to our age, don't we?'

Nina Tanya stands behind Maria's chair so they can both see the other in the same mirror, bulbs all blown in the lights all around it and I'm looking deep down inside my make-up bag like I'm not even listening.

Tanya bends down to flick Maria's jewelled earring.

Tanya 'The thing is, I didn't even do it for the money. Truth be told, I let him do it because I was bored. See, I'd rather be a whore, at least then I get some action. I know you get plenty of satisfaction from thinking I'm embarrassed, but that night in booth number two, I came twice.

When's the last time that happened to you?'

Nina Maria holds her stare glares so hard I think the glass might crack, then she smiles, Tanya pats her on the back and we all get back to normal.

Right on cue, Steve the manager heaves himself through the dressing-room door.

Steve 'Girls, none of you better have any stage calls. If you miss it, you're missing – remember that now. It's a fifty quid fine no dillydallying or complaining it's taken straight out your money. What's so funny?'

Nina Tanya's laughing and lighting a fag under the no-smoking sign, her very hard nipples showing through her tight transparent top from where she got an ice cube and rubbed them earlier, says it gives her good luck.

Tanya 'D'ya want your cock sucked, Steve, is that why you're in here?'

Steve   'No thanks, Tan, there's some versions out there of you twenty year ago so that'll do from your mouth for tonight. Just checking everything's alright as it's nearing 1 a.m. and I ain't seen you out there yet. Get a move on. It's looking busy, you girls could have a good un. Don't get lazy, ladies.'

Nina   And he leaves, I feel lucky that he hardly even notices me.

I don't speak enough and I think he only likes blondes really anyway. Tanya and Maria gossip about the rumours they've heard that he's been seen in a gay club and I do my finishing touches, smudging eyes to look a bit pissed and backcombing hair to look like I just got kissed against a wall – which never seems to happen to me anymore – one spray of Dior and I'm out of the door and into the soft-lighted scene of scented flesh and azure clouds of dry ice above emerald lasers.

The credit-card machines gleam in the corners and I feel so excited, cos it's like a treasure chest, if you can open it.

I sit on one of the leather stools facing the stage, order a fruit punch and dangle, looking attractively drunk, waiting for a punter to come take the bait.

Instead, as soon as I turn my head a young girl who's worked here near on a year leans close to my ear so I can hear her teenage voice poised with a question though there's no question I can answer with this disaster mix tape of Now 48 'No no no-no-no-no no-nono-no no no there's no limit' playing so loud in the background.

So we move round to an empty booth, which we shouldn't do but I pretend I'm helping her tie up the frayed black ankle ribbon on her too high too tight shoes. Her legs are porcupined with pinpricks of orange bits, the holes where the stubble grows showing her spray tan.

Her hands are small. She's got sovereigns on three fingers but I don't bother to say I didn't think people wore them anymore. She's got a scar on her cheek like a claw from a bear tore at her flesh but she shows me her best side and says through lips that men here would tip hundreds to have brought near their dicks:

Young Girl   'What do these lot want from me? Tell me cos I know you know. I ain't making all that much cash in fact I'm losing and it don't feel nice. You've been ere nuff time you got your flow all worked out you got a circuit no one can touch you got –'

Nina   Soft eyes. She had proper soft eyes.

And I wanted to reply, I wanted to say it's not a game with rules like that, babe, you got to find your own way, but for a start try and get a real tan; take off those rings, bring in some diamantes – just not on your teeth.

Never tell the truth, they don't want you, they want another one and besides, they don't deserve it.

Stay strong no matter who tries to stick their finger in your arse mid-dance and don't suck the manager's cock cos that'll never stop you from having to work weekends anyway. Smile a lot, that's the top tip I can give.

Smile no matter what they say, smile all you can, someone your age could have them old geezers, the sleazes, eating right out ya hand.

But I can't. Instead I say:

'Why don't you leave this place?

You've got a gorgeous face you could go anywhere you wanted.

This is it you know this is your one life your one time to make it yours make it right make it something that exists for more than a stag night or a bar fight or a tight-arse CEO's birthday party.

You got to grab it now, mighty fast cos before you know it years have passed and life, the one life you get given, has shrivelled and the pinnacle of your career has been a twist on the pole and there's a big hole where so much else could've been –'

The girl leans closer.

Young Girl   'Sister, I'm alright.

I'm studying creative writing at college at night right before I come here.

I'm just getting some paper for me and my son before my proper time comes.'

Nina   The soft eyes look me up and down.

Young Girl   'But what about you?'

Nina   And I say,
'I'm due on stage now, love,
but take care,
I'll see you around'.

End.

Clean

Clean was written in many different stages. It was originally a short poem I performed as part of an event at Battersea Arts Centre which led them to invite me to work on expanding it as a solo performance piece during a development week at the venue. I didn't get it to a place I was happy with during that week so left the idea and the characters alone until Orla O'Loughlin, at that time artistic director of Traverse Theatre in Edinburgh, who had seen the Old Vic New Voices play I'd taken to Edinburgh Fringe that year, *One Hour Only* (2012), invited me to write a 'Dream Play'. The Dream Plays were fifteen minutes of a play you thought you'd never get to write, to be produced the following week at the Traverse during the third week of the festival. It was a huge opportunity but as there were only 48 hours to write something I didn't think I could do it – on the other hand, I was broke and there was a decent fee attached so I said yes and happily remembered my three languishing 'clean criminal' women. I speedily wrote them into a three-hander and on it went. It was received well and was recommissioned as a longer piece for Glasgow's Oran Mor and Traverse's great daytime theatre project, A Play, a Pie and a Pint. I extended the play, with difficulty as I'd really conceived of it as very short form, into the version printed below and it eventually transferred to New York's Off-Broadway, which was a great experience but also made me excited to return next to a solo performer piece, which I did with *Chef*...

Clean opened in Edinburgh at the Traverse Theatre as part of the Traverse's Breakfast Plays season at the Edinburgh Fringe Festival, on 14 August 2013 wih the following cast and creatives:

Chloe	Jade Anouka
Katya	Chloe Massey
Zainab	Emma Dennis Edwards

Director	Orla O'Loughlin
Assistant Director	Bella Loudon
Producer	Traverse Theatre

Characters

Chloe
Katya
Zainab

There are three young women standing on stage or in the audience. These women are **Zainab** *(twenty-three, British Egyptian, London street accent);* **Chloe** *(twenty-nine, black British, London posh accent);* **Katya** *(twenty-five–thirty-five, any ethnicity, soft Russian accent). They are all dressed impeccably and expensively. They mean business.*

Sabrina *(or narrator) comes on audio to introduce the show.*

The Intro

Sabrina 2011, Edinburgh Festival. The Fringe. I'm in it, got a solo show. Do alright. Twenty-four nights of repeating myself when I'm not even pissed. Have lists of shows I've seen and loved. But, I also met a man who wrote the stories for some very well-known computer games. The exploits are famous – accused of inciting violence, rape, robbery and misogyny. So my question is simple – how come all the female characters were so rubbish in these games? No shock at this, asked a lot, got an easy answer. So? 'So, like, girls don't really have adventures do they? I mean, not those type of adventures. I mean, if you want to go themed that's different – like Lara Croft – but not just everyday, street-crime type of happenings, you know?'

This pissed me off lots. Not really cos I thought girls should be valued for their contribution to street-crime type of happenings – but cos I thought he was so posh he'd probably never even been inside a McDonald's, let alone known any boys who'd had 'those types of adventures' either.

Prejudice? Yes. But mine was only matching his so I thought – with this play I'd like to refute this claim. I want to write a tale of three females who could easily be the basis of crime-based computer games and bring hundreds of 'those type of adventures' out of their designer handbags before you can say no male leads, no themes, just everyday "clean crime" type of happenings'.

So see, I searched through the back catalogue of foggy nights out and stories heard and tricks learnt and things done and scams begun and letters written and nails bitten and there they were –

Zainab Zainab –

Chloe Chloe –

Katya Katya.

Zainab   I'm Zainab, twenty-three, baby of the group. I still lives at home and make my mum *mollokaya shurba* – a vegetable soup – just like Gran used to do in Cairo. Occasionally I'll throw money in my little brother's face to get him off my case. He's been brainwashed by our dad that he can have a say in my life, even though he's not even twenty-one. Dad's gone now though, so I teach him the new way.

'Stay out of my way yeh, Mo, don't say anything if you ain't got anything nice to say and take that money there, pay for some tracksuit that fits you, not licks the floor with its bagginess, you tramp.'

Stamp up the stairs. Wear Egyptian gold, some of the bits that didn't get sold to pay for Daddy's debts and get ready – Prada boots, Gucci scarf, skinny jeans – swear they never felt this skinny before tho – fitted silk shirt – all black. Jump into my black BMW M6 Coupé parked outside the maisonette where I'll come back to in the morning and yawn. Roll down the blacked out window to get some air. One last under-scarf check of my thick black hair and keys in. Foot on the pedal. Automatic so no big meddling. Fling scarf off head to thread through belt loops. IPod in. Start to sing. Bring in some new lyrics, bits that sit nicely on my MACced up lips:

(*Singing.*) Zainab. Twenty-three. Rolling in my BMW coupé yeh don't watch me – (*to someone walking outside of the car*) what the fuck, bruv? Watch where you're going yeh? I can see you got a kid with you. Should be in bed anyhow. And I ain't a girl, I'm a woman yeh. (*Kisses teeth.*)

Chloe   A woman now. That's how I, Chloe, see myself. Twenty-nine this year. Time to start thinking big.

I sit in Chelsea, watching these monstrosities of modernity rise all around me and I hate them, but thank them as they make my Peabody council-estate buildings look like they couldn't possibly cost less than a grand a week. Unless you peek inside and see the notices about job-centre opening times and support for refugees, then it would seem that actually this building is one for those from old money, not no money, paying £75 a week with a view of the brown river and the annual flower show. Although, in a way, I am old money. I grew up rather rich, Mummy lost it all, we got moved here and now I've made it all back and have so far lacked the desire to leave this place, but as I say, this is the time, this is the year to start thinking big, to want it, whatever it is, more of it, the best of it. I deserve it, I work for it, I want it, whatever it is.

I got mugged when I was fourteen – for a Nokia you could just about play Snake on and a Karen Millen bag with a dress in it for my mum's birthday. Never been the same since. Sounds dramatic, but I took that shit seriously. Nobody was going to do that to me again. Became a black belt in everything and let life in clean crime 'I would never hurt anybody who didn't deserve it' begin. Now I slide into the side of my X5 and switch on the seat heat, it's a bit chilly, the air's got a bite. Foot on the pedal, driving into the night, on the way to find what I want.

Katya   Not much is known about my history. I am too young to be ex-KGB. But then some say they had child spies brought up fluent in five languages and pre-programmed to understand just how to bring down the West so who knows? I certainly have nose for bringing things down. And I am known all over town for my ability to dodge camera phones. I never pose for photos, if there's no proof of what I ever looked like then how I do look now is the best, yes?

Anyway, back to now. Now I have my back to the door of my Mayfair floor-three apartment. Walk. Press button. Elevator. In. Down, three, two, one. The lobby is dented with bite marks of other girl heels, not mine – I wear steel-capped leather boots up to knee. They look shiny and sweet but they smash skull in blink. Not that I do this. I wink at porter. He has five-year-old daughter who come in sometime and I buy her Haribo, Tangfastic so I can steal all the fizzy cherries. I leave. Get into low-rise Maserati waiting outside and jump in beside guy I meet every night.

He say 'hi'. Hand me a pack of playing cards. Ace of spades, queen of hearts – then, ones written with fake details of fake accounts of fake money that becomes real in my hands. He goes bit pale. Did I like the joke? I poke him in ribs. 'Let me tell you this. If any of these turn out to be less than 10k like last time, I have no problem to cut off your dick and tie around your neck.'

He smiles, I think he happy that I think it can be long enough to do that with – his neck is very thick. He drop me off to where I need to be, the restaurant, to meet, to eat, to be.

The Restaurant

Zainab   The restaurant is like, mostly white. There are some neon bits of brightly coloured wall, no windows so you dunno if it's night or day. But it's mostly night.

The people who are dining here are mostly right and they all seem to be of a strangely similar height. The club that I been doing business in for a year or so now, the club that I love, the club where I near enough live, is just there, through the restaurant back door.

This place is one of them ones that has never had to throw out a punter for fighting before and the lobby's lighting fixture cost much more than some people in some countries sell their sisters for, serious. The man who opens the door is mostly someone who worked for the royal family once before. I'm sitting on the VIP second floor as I know one of the owners, who mostly owns football teams that never score – but he wanted a place to entertain and so he did what most people with too much money do and opened a restaurant stroke club which is mostly white for people who are mostly right and all seem to be of a, like, strangely similar height.

Right now, my business date is late. The owner's put me in a good place though, spaced so I can like, check out the faces on display. I'm mainly checking these two clean-crime ladies, that's my category as well, clean crime – meaning no death no blood no mess kinda ting but still illegal as sin.

Anyways, I see these two, Chloe and Katya, but they ain't seen me. Which is how it should be, cos I ain't one of them ones who wants to be seen. Not like that Chloe, gleaming all over with diamonds and shit like someone's gonna find that discreet. She treats people like they ain't worth her words – I mean, I never met her, but I heard. And I can see the way her back so straight in her chair, is like she trying so hard to get her nose higher in the air. Yeh, she ain't subtle boy. But I hear she's good at what she does so I ain't fussing, just, I'd never be trusting someone who wore their work round their neck, ya get me?

Chloe   I just don't get people sometimes. I absolutely know that to me, emerald smuggling is everything. You know how those chavs who love to sing go on *X Factor* and say, 'if I don't get through to the next stage, my life is over'? Yes, well it's quite like that for me as I approach the automatic customs doors at airports, painted-nail fingers digging into my luggage handle as the belt with the home-made dents for the uncut emeralds sits comfortably on the waist of my skin-tight jeans. As soon as the doors open, I re-crown myself queen of clean crime and bless the gleamy green stones for being as conflict-free as my fair-trade detox tea. You see, they're not like diamonds, emeralds don't hurt anybody. Indeed I go out of my way to ensure I work in a world where nobody is getting hurt.

Zainab   I flirt with the waiter, no harm done. Turn to watch Katya now. On the other side of the mostly white room chews food like she about to spit it out on somebody's face. She got eyes laced with ice, that's right, she's cold as where she comes from, I can see. Don't know too much bout her history. No one does. She's way too young to be ex-KGB but some say they had child spies brought up fluent in five languages and pre-programmed to understand just how to bring down the West so who knows? All I know is that I see her give a fly kick to some dick in a suit outside a club once and I told her 'nice one' and she shock me cos I didn't think she knew me but she turned and her icy eyes smile and she goes –

Katya   Thank you, Zainab. Keep staring at me, please, make me feel clean, yes, make me feel . . . famous. It is sweet how she think I don't see. She think eyes must meet eyes to know eyes are there. She has wonderful hair. Her stare is – angry. I hear she is the best at what she does. Highest credit limits, infinitely superior quality plastics. Details on cloned cards raised just right, not afraid to fight – for what is hers, what is right, what is wrong. Me and she, we would get along. But she is so very young and too arrogant I think from the way she sink in her chair like she does not care who is watching or waiting. In future, maybe we work together. Now, I stay away, will be trouble to work with one so young.

Bubbles in my glass nearly flat, where is the –

Chloe   Waiter?

Katya   One more please –

Zainab   Please bring the bill, boss –

Chloe   So, as I was saying, I don't understand what is wrong with some people. My clients always get what they ask for from me – always. So it is rather infuriating to sit here and be asked questions about how I do what I do how I find what I find how I know what I know, who can validate my claims – well, mister, my fame as the best emerald smuggler of recent years is surely why you're sitting here? It is me who should be interrogating you. But I don't say this, as business has been less than busy these past few months so, instead I offer statistics on my performance. Never caught, never not delivered, never driven by anything other than getting the job done. He seems impressed, I'm ready to leave, but his eyes linger on my chest longer than they should and I think about shooting my spiked-heel foot into his crotch. But I don't.

Katya   I don't understand why she stare at me, that Chloe –

Chloe   And why won't that bloody bitch stop staring at me, like some kind of commy spy? I stare back, but she lacks the courage for a face-on attack. I consider walking up to her, this icy-eye cutting has gone on far too long, I have no idea what it is *I'm* supposed to have done wrong.

I ignore this Katya's cheap stare for now. My new client, well he is a sleaze, but he offers me a bottle of Cristal down in the club. I adore Cristal more than I abhor a sleaze so I say yes please and off we go.

The Bathroom

Zainab   I go to the bathroom before the club. Business date never turned up so I'm up for seeing what's up downstairs. Check that the scarf that'll be tucked tight around my hair when I go back home is thrown around my neck now in a way that says like, chic Paris, not cheap Primarni – cos that ain't me, no way. This here is Gucci – no big logo tho, cos I ain't a wannabe. Kiss the mirror, this girl here wannabe having an adventure tonight, yagetme?!

Katya   I want to be happy tonight. Life is short. My dinner date did not pass the test so he goes, I will only work with those I trust 100 per cent. I know some investors down in the club, so I do my shirt button up one and decide the night must go on. Quick check in toilet mirror, pass her, Zainab –

Katya *and* **Zainab**   Hello.

Katya   Do lipstick, flick kohl on icy eyes. Surprise toilet attendant by having my own mouthwash. I tell her 'trust nobody in this town' and she nods as I tip her five pound.

The Club

Chloe   You *must* tip the waitress in a club, I tell my new client – but he is useless. I can only guess how he has so much bloody money with so little bloody manners. Hardly matters nowadays – although perhaps it never did, I suppose. He throws me off guard as he unfurls his lips and asks; 'Who's that beautiful young girl?'

Zainab   I see that Chloe in the club with pearls in her ears – real no doubt about that – looking at me as she sits with some fat twat in a too-tight suit and I think yesss, he looks like a prime clone ranger, boi! I bet he's got a black AmEx, yep, me can taste it. Unlimited credit. Now he's proper eyeing me up, so any doubt I had about fleecing him is gone like fuck it, this is it, I'm going over, sticking that turned up nose of hers and that fat face of his in my –

Katya   Shit. What is it? The bouncer – who I do not like because he try one time to tell me I could not wear such big solid spikes on my boots – even though he knew who I know and knew who I am – this bouncer taps my shoulder. Now he tells me the one he knows I know – the co-owner of the club I am in, Caitlin, she wants to see me, upstairs in the office immediately. I down my whiskey, hand him my empty glass and go.

Chloe   Go to the office, the bouncer says, in a way that makes me want to smash the champagne bottle in his pumped up chest. The girl is walking over now, the beautiful young girl with a walk too confident to be un-criminally funded and my client is blinded, not minding at all that I'm about to leave him to go and speak with Caitlin. We agree a date, a price, a place and I follow the bouncer up to Caitlin, it has been a while . . .

Zainab   It's been a while, still, since I been ready to go do this small thing myself. Like, to get into stealth mode, grab a PIN code, throw hair over shoulder, laugh loads as I tell bad jokes, say you're a nice bloke, give your arm a stroke as my other hand takes the card out the machine as you've paid for my drink, wraps it up in your receipt, little detail-stealing contraption flat on my palm, inaudible beep – it's done. I thank you for the drink, say I have to run, be back in a bit. Slip to the car, sync the machine to the Mac, send that through to my crew along with the PIN I stole with my grin, pick up the new plastic on the way home. Use that in the morning to throw thousands around town like it's a Lotto win.

These days I get others to do all this, I sit and direct it all, get my cut, be the boss. So, I'm excited, feels nice to be back where I started. But then my heart beats quick as my favourite bouncer intercepts me as I see one approach that Chloe too and he tells me I gotta go upstairs to see Caitlin, but she don't even know me I say and he say well, maybe she wants to and I go to the stairs to the office and I see them there –

The Office

Chloe   Chloe.

Katya   Katya.

Zainab   Zainab.

Chloe   Nice to meet you both, finally.

Katya   Anyone like drink?

Zainab *and* **Chloe**   No.

Zainab   I don't drink.

Chloe   I do. I just don't trust you.

Zainab   Woah.

Katya   You. *You* don't trust *me*? This is so funny.

Chloe   Really?

I'm about to ask why as I know humour is not what I'm known for, but Caitlin walks through the door and we all take leather seats which seem to make us sink, so we all sit up straight one –

Zainab   Two –

Katya   Three –

Chloe   As I wonder what the hell Caitlin wants with me –

Zainab   And so this co-owner lady, this famous clean-crime legend, she tells us she knows we're the best at what we do and she needs us to help her take some well-deserved revenge and make some serious paper –

Katya   I have so much spare 'paper' I buy the entire left side of a river in Latvia. I don't need money and somebody else's revenge sounds like somebody else's business, I am not interested. I am about to say this, when–

Chloe   Kristof –

Katya   Kristof Clementine?!

Chloe *and* **Katya**   No!

Zainab   Who?

Katya   I pace. Mind races at the mention of this name. The shame –

Chloe   How I ever allowed such a man to embarrass me, to make me feel ashamed –

Zainab   I can't claim I have a clue who this dude is, but at the mention of his strange-sounding name these two go a bit doolally and I'm like what did he –

Katya   He betrayed me, in the beginning, when I need a good guide. Everybody lies in this world, in this business, of course, but he, he went too far –

Chloe   He bloody didn't go far enough for me!

Zainab   Caitlin says she knows how he treated them both, how he told Chloe he loved her and then left her, stood her up to cosy up with an older old money lady from the south of France –

Chloe   I've been waiting for this moment for years –

Zainab   How he reduced hard-eyed Katya to tears by kidnapping her sister so he could wrestle a ransom of diamonds from her –

Katya   And you, Caitlin, I remember what he did to you. Opening that rival club and stealing some of your best workers and customers –

Zainab   Caitlin says how she never forgave him for bribing her staff, she looks after her people, but people are greedy and she took it very personally. I'm a bit confused and I say:

But what about me? I've never even heard of this Kristof Clementine dude –

Chloe   The less you say his name, the better, Zainab –

Zainab   Caitlin says she's seen me, she can see I'm hungry, I agree and she says she needs me, my skills in identity fraud will be very useful for the plan ahead –

Katya   There is no question about it, revenge on him is priceless, I nod my head –

Chloe   I nod my head, I want to hurt him, I am in –

Zainab   I am so excited, I nod my head like I'm on speed and I'm in we're in and we all agree to the plan that we know fuck all about we just trust Caitlin knows what she's on about and then Katya and Chloe look about from me to each other and back to Caitlin as she says we will be together, just us three, that's the plan, that's the way it has to be –

Katya   I hate him, I really do. I want to help you, I really do, but –

Katya *and* **Chloe**   I always work alone.

Zainab   I dunno what their problem is, but they shut it quick when Caitlin explains that as well as get revenge, they'll get enough emeralds and diamonds to retire on and I'll leave holding the details of identities that will set me up as the best in the field, globally. The only thing she wants from it all is one tiny little computer chip.

Katya   I sit and I think. This could be it. The final job. The one to get me what I want. I do not want to work with anyone, but –

Chloe My mind runs in circles. I know this could be the one, the job to get me what I want, to be where I want. I really do not want to work with anyone, but . . .

Zainab They bite their lips, they slit their eyes, sigh, nod their heads, finally, they are definitely in, Caitlin smiles. We climb into a car, roar onto a runway, pile into a private jet, take off, night sky, leave the stars behind.

The Private Jet

Katya *is napping.*

Chloe I'm making a drink – sure you don't want one?

Zainab I don't drink. I told you.

Chloe I see.

Zainab What exactly does she do? Katya?

Chloe Market manipulation to the highest degree, apparently. Uses fake company accounts to buy up shares, which sends the prices sky high whilst she sells her real shares at its peak. By the time they find out the buying companies were frauds, insurance pays and nobody's hurt.

Zainab Seen. Sounds pretty sick to me. We're both into a similar thing then.

Chloe Hmm. She also runs a diamond smuggling ring, but it's really having minimal impact, a bit of a bad joke if you ask me. Why don't you drink?

Zainab Why do you think you're too good to work with me?

Chloe Zainab, I don't work with anybody. I work alone.

Zainab But you don't. You were sat there in that club with some fat twat in a too-tight suit and he –

Chloe He is a client. I don't work with him. For him. It's different. I have to work *for* somebody, I don't have to work *with* anybody.

Zainab   Well, I don't work for no one –

Chloe   Everybody works for someone, dear –

Zainab   Listen, I'm a grown woman and I don't work for nobody yeh, out ere on my own, ya get me.

Chloe   Hmm, I see.

Zainab   Do you though?

Chloe   Well, right now, we're all working for Caitlin –

Zainab   And working together –

Chloe   Apparently yes, so there's a first for all of us I suppose, dear –

Zainab   I'm about to say stop 'dearing' me yeh like I'm some little kid, I AM A GEE – but then Katya gets up from her nap and puts the plans for the plan in our laps and says –

Katya   Let's get to work. When we know what we have to do, we can all go back to being on our own –

Chloe   Excellent, can't wait –

Zainab   The plans are laid out, complicated but clear –

Katya   We arrive as staff at his daughter's big birthday party –

Zainab   I make the identities for us as soon as we land –

Katya   We have earpiece to stay in touch, so I tell you what people are saying –

Zainab   I get a fingerprint from Kristof's champagne glass –

Chloe   I get the code for the safe from his phone –

Katya   I keep watch –

Zainab   I grab the identity documents and the computer chip for Caitlin from the safe –

Chloe   Sorry, but does anyone know what is so great about this one little chip?

Katya   Yes, I hear. Kristof is such stupid dick. He want everyone to think he is coolest man and so he pay millions to develop new computer game, best ever graphics, gory hardcore violence, it will make billions. He release it next week and everything is on there all there, on that chip –

Zainab   And that's it? No back-up?

Katya   No. It was too top secret to chance it.

Katya   Caitlin have someone who sleeps with his personal bodyguard for a while, he find out things.

Zainab   So losing this game will hurt him more than anything else –

Katya   Yes, he think this is his route to real fame, outside of the crime game.

Chloe   Anyway, back to the plan. So then, I get the stones from the safe –

Katya   No, I get the stones –

Chloe   I think you'll find I should do that –

Katya   It does not say you here on the plan –

Chloe   Neither does it say you –

Katya   I know Caitlin better –

Chloe   I know stones better –

Katya   Only emeralds –

Chloe   Only *everything*. I just choose emeralds to be my –

Katya   You are too scared for diamonds –

Chloe   Actually, I don't agree with where they come from –

Katya   Oh please –

Chloe   You don't have the class to carry emeralds, Katya –

Katya   I carry nothing, others do it for me, Chloe –

Chloe   Exactly, no pride in the job, no sacrifice –

Katya   You should catch up with the times –

Chloe   I am twenty-nine years old, thank you, I am very much of the time and I won't be told by a –

Zainab   Maybe you two should calm it yeh, we all gotta get on for this shit, just squash the beef yeh –

Chloe   YOU can't even speak English and SHE is undercutting all my years' worth of hard work so NO, the 'beef', so to speak, is certainly not to be 'squashed'!

*Zainab, **Chloe** and **Katya** all go off in a huff to different corners of the plane. Alone. Asleep?*

The Van

*Zainab, **Chloe** and **Katya** are huddled in the back of a van, an ex-Soviet state.*

Zainab   Now, four hours later, far from home and so far from being alone we three – Zainab –

Chloe   Chloe –

Katya   Katya –

Zainab   Are sat in the back of a sorta van, on the way to see some sorta man who's sposed to sort us out with some sorta equipment for us to carry out some sorta plan. The tension is high, I think sparks might fly –

Chloe   This is not the type of transport I'm used to, it's quite ridiculous –

Zainab   Katya just sort of hisses, she's not yet used to this proximity –

Katya Just as this Chloe is about to say something she regret to me, the van screech to stop –

Zainab I ain't got my belt on so my face is squashed up on the window as it leans to one side like the tyres have gone –

Chloe My side of the van door opens and –

Katya The driver's on the road with hole in his head, though we hear no shots –

Chloe I'm not prone to violence generally, but I hate the sight of blood and it's bleeding all over the tarmac, his head, so I take the knife from the heels of my boot –

Zainab Chloe's got her knife out –

Katya Please, what will that do?

Zainab So Katya gets out a Glock from her sock and it's all getting on top but I kinda like it kinda and I'm also completely shitting it but I put on a brave face like yeh, I like this, I like it –

Chloe I don't like how quiet it is.

Zainab Quietly, I sneak outside, but suddenly arms grab me –

Chloe I see Zainab in trouble so I jump out, my knife out, don't want to use it but I will –

Katya It is a long time since I've killed, I don't want to now. But how else to help? I elbow the attacker in the neck –

Zainab I'm crying like a kid and without batting an eyelid Katya lashes the dude around the head with her gun –

Chloe We start to run but gloved hands grab my throat –

Zainab And again, Katya comes jumping in, pulls Chloe away and the figure is down down down on the ground so we run again.

But soon there's a car in front of us, blacked out windows like I got on my coupé –

Katya   I fire shot but they bounce back. Bullet-proof –

Chloe   Absolute fools to come here, who cares that he dumped me, stood me up, whatever and who cares about stashes in safes I don't want to retire anyway –

Zainab   No one can say anything else as we each get an arrow in the arm and feel so . . . dreamy and sleepy and one –

Chloe   Two –

Katya   Three.

They fall asleep.

The Warehouse

Zainab, **Chloe** *and* **Katya** *are in a concrete warehouse. They are sitting down on crates.*

Chloe   How long have we been in here now? This blacked-out grey building with not a place to be alone in. Shivering.

Katya   I feel at home.

Chloe   No you don't.

Katya   I do. Are you going to say thank you?

Chloe   For what?

Katya   Saving you.

Chloe   Saving? To end up in here? Can you hear this, Zainab?

Zainab   You did save us both still, safe for that, although, Chloe, you surprised me too, jumping in there you know, but Katya – that elbow you got –

Katya   Not a problem.

Chloe   I've got a problem. With you, Katya.

Zainab   The grey walls of the place we're in are spiky with cement and the feelings being vented seem to reflect the environment and we got no clue what we're sposed to do an I don't want them to fight but they gotta get it out sometime so –

Katya   So, what it is? This problem?

Chloe   What have I done to you to make you stare at me like I've given you some fatal disease? I don't care to be friends, but I do care to know, as who knows how long we'll be here.

Katya   Your fear makes you brave to ask this as –

Chloe   No! My boredom spurs me to, I was ready to walk straight up to you and ask outright the other night but –

Katya   You didn't.

Chloe   No. So?

Katya   Ok. I look at you because you look at me and I wonder what your problem is why you stare with this look of hate at me –

Chloe   Well, that's easily answered –

Katya   Really?

Chloe   Yes. I look at you because you piss me off with your cheap prices –

Katya   My what?!

Chloe   You charge less for your smuggling trips than I do, you send inexperienced workers out and it gives us a bad name, it makes me have to explain why my price is higher –

Katya   *You* give us a bad name, the way you put nose in the air and act like you are better than even the client who pay you. This makes enemies for us, they think we think we are above our place –

Chloe   Our place? This is what I mean, Katya. You act as if we owe them something. We owe them nothing except the stones they pay for –

Zainab   Do both of you make alright money?

Katya *and* **Chloe**   Yes.

Zainab   Then it's cool, innit? Enough to go round. No need to hate . . . Look yeh, this could be make or break out here, we win – no one is gonna mess with either of you about anything, you're gonna run whatever you want to. We lose – that Clementine dude gets to laugh at you again and word gets about, no doubt the whole scene would bust out the giggles, let us wriggle for jobs like any little newbies. So let's just admit it, we're on the same side, yeh?

Pause.

Chloe   You do have impressive reflexes, Katya.

Katya   Thank you. You have impressive client lists.

Chloe   Right, well. Thanks.

Zainab   I see Katya's eyes unfreeze and it's a little bit scary cos she's actually got a nice face but it's always so hard and then she starts to laugh and I'm confused I dunno what has really just gone on but like, the tension in this grey concrete box has diffused a bit and I'm sitting just thinking what –

Katya   What shall we have drink? I think they leave vodka here for us. A favourite in this part of world.

Chloe   Yes, please.

Katya   So now you trust me?

Chloe   If you do me.

Zainab   Just water please. I don't drink. Don't you think, like, it's a bit dodgy to drink some any kinda drink they jus left here after they shot us? It might be like, poison or summin.

Katya If they like to poison they would kill when we asleep. They not, so not want to kill us. Want us to survive. So we drink. It will help.

Chloe We sit.

Katya We drink.

They begin to drink.

Zainab Them two *drink,* boi.

Some time passes quietly, drinking. Singing? Tapping beats on crates?

Chloe I think it was the first time I did a modelling shoot I puked from doing shots of straight vodka with the photographer who said it would loosen me up. Turned out he had other tools in mind to loosen me up with at the end of the night. So I bought him a flaming sambuca from the bar and pushed it in his eyes. He nearly went blind.

Katya When I was a child, the snow in winter so bright I nearly blind. We hold on to rope to go school, pull along with skis. I miss these days, best time of my life.

Chloe Really? Gosh I hated school, childhood really, the whole lot of it. I do, however, remember the best time of my life. It was only my third time smuggling emeralds. I got off the first-class flight in JFK and went straight to a limo, straight to champagne, straight to being paid enough to buy my own car and the client looked at the flat cloudy uncut jewels in the flat of my hand and said, 'I never thought a woman like you could do that'. It was then that I knew – it wasn't the money, though that is sensational – it was that I could do what would never be expected of me and excel in it, dwell in it, get rich in it, live in this world of late-night clubs and lay-down flight seats and gourmet eating, meeting the richest and most powerful in the world and knowing that even they can't do what I do. They wouldn't even try. I think I'd rather die than give it up.

Zainab I get up to stretch my legs. The vodka has made them two loose-lipped and that's cool I don't mind but I'm not about to start telling them all the things on my mind, but there's kinda a lot right now. So I walk around the mostly grey room. No windows so you can't tell if it's night or day. I guess it's mostly night. I think about how tight my mother's face went when my dad left all his debts, abandoned her to be alone now, and I get angry at myself now for being here, not there with her at home wonder what the fuck are we waiting for I kick the metal door hard like I wanna break my foot, I think I might break my foot –

Chloe   Zainab! You'll break your foot! What are you doing?

Zainab   What are *we* doing though? Sitting around like it's story time? It's time to get the fuck out of here, I wanna leave –

Katya   And go where?

Zainab   Don't care. Not just sitting here like some mug waiting for them there to come back and shoot us with more than drugged arrows.

Chloe   I have to say I do agree. Although let's maybe discuss it less aggressively –

Zainab ignores me and gets a small metal machine from underneath her bra. She starts using the corner of it to try and unscrew the bolts on the door –

Katya   I decide, finally, that I really do like these two. I help try to unscrew the bolts with the spikes from my boots –

Chloe   My knife is twisting as I try to unblock the padlock –

Zainab   My fingertips are cut –

Katya   I wish I had my Glock, they took it, but I don't stop twisting the spike –

Chloe   I try and try we heave and sigh and then –

Zainab   It slides –

Katya   The door opens and we find –

Chloe   No outside scene of trees and fields like we thought there'd be –

Zainab   A pair of Jimmy Choo heels in front of my face –

Chloe   My face faces manicured toenails that kick my knife to the side as it falls –

Katya   My mouth falls open –

Zainab   Her eyes wide open, Caitlin smiles and says that like, she's glad to see us –

Katya   And I ready to fight her, but I remember that she is leading us to revenge on the man I hate more than anything –

Chloe   But this is too much. Caitlin is evidently touched in the head and I stand up straight, about to announce that I'll be getting away, I don't really care either way for this revenge any longer but I remember I don't know the way where we are who knows I don't know what is going on –

Zainab   What is going on, Caitlin says, is that she watched us on the CCTV on the plane and in the van and she realised she would have to change up the plan as she couldn't have us all not getting along. She just wanted us to have a proper, close introduction to each other. Now that this seems to be done, she can see how well we all get along –

Katya   She wants us to all get along –

Chloe   We could have got along in London with a game of poker for God's sake this is taking the –

Zainab   I nearly piss myself with excitement, anger, I dunno, as she goes that we should all sit down together, start to really put the plan together, we have work to do.

The Plan

Zainab   The house is like, mostly white. There are some neon bits of brightly coloured wall, no uncovered windows so you dunno if it's night or day. But it's mostly night. The people who are partying here are mostly right and they all seem to be of a strangely similar height. The club that I love is not downstairs. There is, however, the safe in the pool engine room down there. I stare at the birthday party guests and see that round here everything glares with bait shit, like people so happy to have money they wanna bathe in it, which I can kinda get, but still, it's a bit much. I hope nobody talks to me as I don't know what they're saying and my earpiece needs turning up. I keep my tray up, take empty glasses back to the kitchen until I see him, Kristof, a blur of black suit oblivious to mostly everything, staring at the pool –

Katya   I take up position by pool, ready to keep watch for security that might try stop Zainab and Chloe doing their work. Earpiece in, whispering translations to those two as they move about. I spill drinks enough to keep me wiping up here for a while. Through the long glass panes, I see it begin –

Chloe   I see him, Kristof. Zainab approaches him like a pro, offers her tray at just the right time, inviting angle. He downs the last sip of his fizz and rests the glass on the tray, not even looking at who it is that holds it, what a God-awful prick he is. She leaves, to unstick his fingerprint from the glass and I begin to saunter over, made over with magnificent marvels of fabric, ready to attack this shit. Although, I have no idea of how this might go –

Zainab   I take the print from the glass like a gangster cos I'm sick like that but still, my hand shakes. I make it to the pool room with the safe and I hope Chloe arrives with the code before someone asks as I can't speak a word of this language and the whispers from Katya in the earpiece are too low to repeat –

Chloe   He looks at me like I'm speaking another language. Which of course I am, in comparison to the bright young things here for his daughter. He is confused, but shows it only slightly, comes in to hug me, I smile and smile and he looks at me in that way of his for enough of a while that I know I can do this, it will be easy –

Katya   She will pull this off easy. Kristof hugs her and keeps his hand on her shoulder. She must be explaining to him how she happened to be in town for business, got an invite from some kid she'd made friends with and he was the last person she expected to see and he is now getting his phone out –

Chloe   His phone out, I touch his chest, whisper in his ear so my lips touch his skin that I remember what happens when I leave things to him and so I take the phone, say I'll put my own number in and I type the numbers and ring the phone Katya has –

Katya   The phone flashes and I answer, a few seconds, enough to let me hack inside, find what I looking for from his phone, downloaded. I text the code to Zainab, Chloe comes closer to her –

Zainab   As Chloe comes behind me I feel bile rising in my throat. The fingerprint has worked, the code is cleared but there's summin Caitlin didn't know and I whisper to Katya on the earpiece that –

Katya   We need his damn iris scan –

Chloe   This is not part of the plan –

Katya   Keep it together, we will find a way –

Chloe   Katya is about to say something but stops and I peek from the side of the pool-room door and I see one of the in-charge staff asking her a trail of questions and she nods and bends her long neck like a swan and she starts to follow him, darts her eyes at the pool room but she can't see me in the dark and then she's gone –

Zainab   Shit, shit, shit, is this it? Is this where we get caught and end up in some freezing cell smelling each other's shit for the next three to five years, hearing about the outside world only when the guards decide to fight over football results and we get one can of spam or summin a day and –

Chloe   Calm down, Zainab. The plan will go on.

I give her one of my mini make-up mirrors and tell her what I'm going to do –

Zainab   What she's going to do is nuts, she's nuts, but what the fuck we ain't got much choice so I stand still and straight and just wait.

Chloe   I have Kristof by the pool. I bring him under a spotlight, I tell him I could dance with him all night. He asks if we could go somewhere more private, I say of course, but oblige my poolside fantasy one moment please and at the mention of fantasy he smiles and although I hate him that smile makes me feel something deep down and I feel slightly guilty for a second and then I remember how much my tears cost and tell him he has something gross in his eye. I get a mirror out, he looks into it, close up, touching his eyelashes, his vanity making him scared to look stupid. The reflection of his eye goes to the mirrored ceiling via the spotlight and I pray that Zainab catches the iris pattern via my angled make-up mirror – one side hooking the reflection and the other reflecting into the scanner –

Zainab   It's only gone and worked! What a motherfucking p.i.m.p. – she just smashed it but now how to be quiet enough, he is right there, so close and I'm like woah, there's a lot of shit in this safe I can't do it myself and I wonder where Katya is, how Chloe is gonna get rid of that dickhead –

Chloe   I tell him I want to come to his room soaking wet – from swimming. I'll meet him there. He couldn't find anything in his eye. I say maybe it was in mine, going blind. Laugh sweetly. He says he'll pick up some champagne, tells me the way. I smile a million okays and can't believe that he leaves and that this might really work –

Zainab   It's worked. Me and Chloe leave the pool engine room safe with no alarm being sparked and our bags full of what we came for and the computer chip is inside my mouth –

Chloe   Doesn't that taste awful Zainab?

Zainab   Ask me later. We need to find Katya.

Chloe   There she is at the front gate, in the midst of a fly kick to a guard –

Katya   He recognise me –

Chloe   Three more guards storm from the house –

Zainab   It's about to blow –

Katya   GO!

Zainab   We run –

Chloe   And run –

Katya   And run –

Zainab   And run –

Chloe   And run –

Katya   And run –

Zainab   And run –

Chloe   And run –

Katya   And run.

Zainab *and* **Chloe** *and* **Katya**   *Overlapping/simultaneous/ excitable –*

We did it! Oh my God that was crazy! Did you see that guard's face?! We are the best, wow, the iris mirror thing was genius, who could have guessed it?! We are absolutely sick. Yes, yes, yes. We got everything. All of it. Every little bit. We are the shit.

The Office II

Zainab   So here we are, Zainab –

Chloe   Chloe –

Katya   Katya –

Zainab   Back in the office where it all began, handing over a tiny computer chip to Caitlin –

Katya   Caitlin is smiling and smiling –

Chloe   She hacked into the CCTV in Kristof's house, to freeze it while we did our thing and now she plays us footage of him crying –

Katya   Crying like baby –

Chloe   Like he made me –

Zainab   He couldn't believe he'd lost it –

Katya   His precious chip –

Chloe   But he's not completely stupid –

Katya   He know it something to do with Chloe –

Chloe   I never went to the room, the number didn't work, I was gone when he emerged in his dressing gown –

Zainab   We think we might all have to leave town, take a new identity, start again and I'm about to say I can't do that, I can't leave my mum, she needs me here, my life is here when –

Chloe   Caitlin begins to burn the chip and the stench of melting metal and plastic is horrific. She's filming it and when it is just a minuscule pile of slimy chemicals she turns the phone around and says, it was me, Kristof, do your worst, presses send.

Zainab   Tells us it's between him and her, we're not to worry, he knows who his war is with.

Chloe   She looks at us, proud, asks us what we plan to do now with our new-found wealth, all the possibilities there must be . . . none of us say anything out loud but –

Katya   I think that this team-work, yes I admit, it is better than I thought. Maybe one day I will do again. Now, it has brought me too close to my past, so when I go home tonight, I pack, I leave, I begin again somewhere new, leave my client list to these two –

Chloe   These two, well, they made me see that I enjoy team spirit at times, that I'm even inclined to find people I like – although I'm not sure I'll have the time to do it again. After I drop a proportion of my jewels over the gate of the local children's home, I will be alone again, not smuggling, but building with bricks in a bit of the world the colour of emeralds, building a home –

Zainab   I'm gonna go home to a family who are sorted now, cos of me. Mum has to be proud, no matter how I did it. Scarf around my hair now . . . but I think nah and take it down again, grown-up Zainab is coming home. How this will go I dunno, but I want less lies in my life, more truth, ya getme? One day I'm gonna be where Caitlin is, yeh, on to level two of this game, that's me – Zainab –

Chloe   Chloe –

Katya   Katya.

The end.

Chef

The idea for *Chef* came about when I was working as a waitress at Ollie Dabbous's first restaurant, Dabbous. The kitchen he ran was so harmonious and choreographed that I was inspired to interview him and the other chefs, hoping to write a restaurant kitchen-based musical. I'd also been working in women's prisons independently facilitating poetry workshops and doing some theatre based ones with the charity Clean Break, so these two seemingly disconnected worlds were at the forefront of my mind. One day, the character of Chef appeared, combining the two worlds and a voice from a performance poem I'd written for an exhibition at the Hayward Gallery about a toxic relationship, which was more personally inspired. It was one of the most exciting creative processes to have these three influences come together in a completely unplanned way. It almost wrote itself, flowing out on my phone, on voicenotes, in a notepad – it found a structure and a rhythm and it was like I just went with it rather than the other way round. I tried out the first scenes at the Basement in Brighton and became confident it could be extended, but for an actor, not for me, as I wanted to really push where it could go emotionally. The director Kirsty Patrick Ward was a huge encouraging force behind the play and we were thrilled to have Jade Anouka come on board to play Chef. Jade really understood the lyricism and what it could do for the story and the audience, bringing so many new layers to the work. I produced this play myself for an Edinburgh Fringe run in 2014 and it was a low-budget, bankrupting thing of chaos. But it won a Fringe First, got nominated for numerous other awards, Jade won The Stage Award for Acting Excellence and to be honest, it was only after this that the work offers I started to get were financially viable enough to consider writing as a full time job. More importantly, it made a real impact in ways I had only hoped it could – being performed at the AGM of UK Prison and Probation

Officers, provoking discussion on treatment of women prisoners, including advocating for therapy focused on working through cycles of violence as something that should be a standardised part of rehabilitation.

Chef was first performed in 2015, with the following cast and creative team:

Chef   Jade Anouka

Writer   Sabrina Mahfouz
Director   Kirsty Patrick Ward
Designer   Fran Reidy
Lighting Designer   Douglas Green
Sound Designer   Edward Lewis

1

Chef *is wearing a white chef's top and jogging bottoms.*

She is the only actor and can be any age and any ethnicity.

She is writing 'The perfect peach' onto a whiteboard.

She lifts a large, cut, dripping peach and holds it out to the audience.

This here, yeh, this is a peach.
A ripe and ready to eat beautiful bit
of meaty peach flesh.
Now listen, right.
If you'd never tasted a peach before –
even like, a metally mouthed one
from a Basics tin or the kind ya find
binded in plastic for lunchboxes or some shit –
then when you finally put this peach
inside your cakehole you would be like,
WOW!
How the fuck did you make that, Chef?
And I could go on, couldn't I?
About how I mixed this ingredient
from an island with a long name,
with another one that was scavenged
from a motorway
not far away from where you was born
and marinated it for a year,
or some such bullshit. But I won't.
Cos I ain't made it, have I?
Life has made it. Mother Earth.
So why hurt perfection?
Why shake it about with flashes of flour
and sparks of sugar,
trying to make it look like a bit of puke
after a good night out?
I mean, what is that about?

Keep it as it is. A bleeding peach.
Just make it the best bleeding peach it can be.
Soak it in its own juice overnight.
Make sure you buy the right ones in the first place.
Organic and that, fresh, you know, no pesticides
or flies finding their homes in its furry fleshy skin.
Put your face right up to its glow and let it know
that you will love it, respect it,
think about how it grew,
before you smash it in your mouth
and munch it quicker than a junkie chick
on a shotter's dick.
But don't be all poncy prick about it,
like you know things no one else could ever know
about this dear sweet little peachy poo.
Cos after all,
a bit later on you'll be saying a 'see you later on'
to it all down the shitter.

Yeh, so that's my, shall we say – philosophy.
On the way I like to do my food, for my guests.
I don't want them to have to guess
what went into what's going into them.
I just do it plain and simple
but so good they never forget it.
Come back every day like they need it to live.
Cos here, they kinda do.
I give a little bit of myself every day to them,
a gift to my loyal guests.
Not literally, obviously,
I mean I don't chop a bit of pinky finger into the pot
or sprinkle dandruff on top of a stew –
let me tell you I ain't got that, by the way,
dandruff, that's proper rough.
I mean, I give from the inside.
Yeh. Trust me, I even got some tough women crying
from what I can do with a lettuce leaf.
As soon as they get that green between their teeth . . .

Well, it's all over.
Who needs diets when veg can taste that good?

This place I'm at now,
they aren't so keen for me to proper experiment,
which is all I want.
All I want really,
it's all I,
it's all that's keeping me going really.
The dream that one day
I'll be able to cook again my way.
Everyone just wants to cook their own way, you know?
And I sometimes think,
you know I used to think it a lot,
when some cocksucker was complaining
about it being too hot
or not hot enough
or it's a bit salty
it's not as fresh as I like
It's got too much sauce,
bit too dry
thought this wasn't fried
are you sure this is organic?
Where are the sides?
Is this all we get?
Haven't you got better bread?
The menu said the menu said the menu said –
FUCK OFF!
I used to think, do you know what this does,
this life?
It cooks. It feeds. It delivers. It delights.
Then it dies.
People just sit there,
take the plate in front of them,
pick at it,
lick the side of a spoon.
Feel no way about pooling groups
of unwanted food

together at the edges
and when it comes back,
where do you think it goes?
We see it,
we see them.
Bulging black bags heaving
with life sustenance that has been rejected,
like the time from my life it took to prepare it
never really mattered.
Like the farmer, the lorry driver, the packer,
like none of us even matter.
How much do you think –
do you think we matter?
Us sorry lot who somehow grow food
or make it palatable,
make it something edible?

Pause. **Chef** *smiles.*

Incredible innit, food?
Couldn't live without it.
But gone so quick,
so unceremoniously.
I think that's why I got into it,
cooking,
eating,
something to put love into
that you don't expect to stick around.
You know it will be gone soon.
Knowing is much much better than hoping,
than supposing.
Knowing it will be gone as soon as it's done,
there's something very comforting about that.
Something comforting about shiny clean surfaces too.
The silver makes me feel safe.
Clean, ya know? I'm very clean, me.
I need to feel cleaner than usual today.
Yesterday,
well something happened here

yesterday,
before dinner service . . .
It was a mess.
I saw the blood.
I didn't make it, it wasn't me, it wasn't mine . . .
I just saw it,
I tried to stop it, stem it,
I wiped it I tried to wipe it – I . . .

2

I loved a man once
who cut shapes into skin cos his words didn't work.
Worst thing was I worked with words,
making up lines for menus, writing reviews for food.
And so when I spoke he looked at me
like I'd hurt a part of him I'd never heard.
I never saw him do it, his work.
But I saw the blood, I wiped it,
dried like a dye-poisoned lake
from the leather of a jacket.
I scrubbed silver Prada trainers doused in DNA
with a bleach-dipped toothbrush
that he'd hardly used.
He wasn't used to a girl like me, he'd say,
Babes, you're so gully you know.
But proper clever too, you wanna do proper things innit?
And I'd smile like yeh, I know, you're right.
Even though every night I used to lie awake,
wonder what the fuck I was gonna do with my life.
Wasn't making enough money writing about food,
I sold some weed here and there but no big thing.
He said he'd bring me in to his shit if I really wanted
but he never did.
He just let me silently do what I always did.
Stroll through the netted smoke he blew,
wrap my legs around his hips and kiss
like my life depended on it.
Cos it sort of did.
If I had actually seen him do it, his work,
maybe I would have left.
Unable to handle the careless mess,
faces like smashed birthday cakes on the pavement.
But then again, maybe I wouldn't.
Because he was sexy and strong
and he made me feel like I was too.
When you've grown up

in a darkness so black it's blue,
that's not something to be taken lightly.
So when one night when he asked me,
Babes, can you put this down your shoe for me yeh?
I say yeh, minor, I was gonna wear boots anyway.
We drive away and I close my eyes,
making my mind as wannabe unsee-through
as the tinted windows on the rented car
that cost more than his flat –
but it was part of all that and he had to have it.
Just like I had to have him, needed him to be happy.
I needed him, to be happy.
After all, this was a world
where a girl could apparently never compete,
the shapes we'd cut into skin
would apparently be too neat,
we'd apparently feel sick
when it really came down to it,
hearing frozen branches of bones crack,
we wouldn't be able to handle that,
wouldn't have that 'thing' it takes
to scrape an eyeball with the edge of a blade
like it's some kind of food's unwanted skin,
bring a knee to a nose, a gun to a tied tongue.
We apparently
just wanted Alize mixed with champagne
and fun wrapped in wraps that never let us forget
who was boss,
how much it cost,
how hard it all was,
to live like this.
We wouldn't want to get our lips bust
because we needed to be looked at
like we were needed to be kissed
and he needed me to feel like this
so that I would need him,
help him feel less empty.
An emptiness that left him so full of soullessness

that he took his own life every night,
There's plenty of ways to die and still stay alive, babes
he used to say.
Anyway, this one night when my Gucci cowboy boots
were full of lead end dreams,
sharp angles that dug into my ankles
making me walk like I had one foot on the moon,
this one night I was standing by a nightclub door,
a loaded gun tucked into my sock
and I spied the possibilities of what I might do.
Like stop a bullet making spirals
through the wiry hair of his chest
by jumping up high,
slow motion hand in action
trigger pulled
but skin cold
as from across the room a bullet pierces me,
making shapes inside no man could make
no matter how much his words didn't work.
And I would die
and he'd be safe, unhurt
and I would die.
I wanted that a little bit, maybe a lot, I'm not sure.
But that isn't what happened at all.
I stood by the nightclub door and I thought,
how does it get to this?
How do kids who want to be astronauts and writers
and singers and engineers end up here?
In the dark corners of someone else's dream,
guarded by thick doors and clipboards,
playing with guns and fists and knives,
forgetting what it was like to be alive once?
They knew once,
before crunches of a system
made them feel that their minds were missing
that nobody would miss them,
that they were dismissed then
from living the type of life others lived . . .

But they would never be forgiven
for not dying trying to live like them.
When
was it ever even possible for us to live like them?

I bent down to get the gun out, ready to say,
I'm out let's duck out,
let's use our money start some sort of business,
it can still be illegal – just not this.
Not violence and conflict,
unpicking the bits of skin that makes up a person,
their memories their existence their reason for being.
Before my hand reaches in,
I see him.
My eye caught a mirror that showed me my life
and it wasn't looking too nice because there he was,
his hand on some girl's face as she faced
the stairs she was going down
and as he turned back around
and saw me looking
his look looked deeper
than if he'd just tried to deny he was inside her,
even though his dick was still in it as he said it.

I left the gun on the desk behind the door,
where the woman on the till
glanced down at it soundlessly
and then straight back to her magazine,
which was screaming about overweight faces
and racist footballers who they'd still marry anyway,
everyone says some things sometimes
that they don't mean, don't they?
I asked her for a pen and she smiled at that,
handed me a black biro. I never gave it back.

I went and sat at the back of a little Chinese place.
Late night type people,
picking their way through Peking duck rolls,
not looking like the night

was worth the extra crow's lines
their eyes would show them in the morning.
I started scribbling a menu
on the back of the crap red napkin.
I thought about the fried food I'd just ate,
that I'd paid for and hated.
I made up some late night convenient dishes,
fresh, simple.
Ran to the 24-hour Asda and made them all at home.
Called my bestie Annie, she came round for breakfast
to taste my late night snacks and she rubbed my back
as I spiced the food with a few tears,
telling me it was the best fucking meal she'd had in years.
She might have just been being nice,
as best mates do when you tell them
the love of your life is a complete prick.
I needed to hear it.
Later on a receptionist at a nice little bistro
near my little flat said the very same thing,
made me come in with samples for the chef
and imagine, he took me on,
taught me to make the things
I'd only written about before.

The chef was a kind man, a family man,
definitely not much of the type of man
I'd had in my life up till then,
his heart as golden as the lemongrass syrup he made.
As soon as I got in there at 7 a.m.
he would take his A4 notepad,
make eight sections in which to break down
into white lined boxes the dish I was learning that day,
explaining the secrets of its complex simplicity to me.
I was in awe of him –
except he didn't believe in baking,
which made my mum tell me to be wary of him.
I was disappointed too,
because baking is what had got me into it all

in the first place as a kid,
seeing that transformation.
Eggs, flour, sugar, butter one minute
and a cake the next.
Something so magical about that.
Whatever you do to meat, it's still meat, isn't it?

I learnt how to taste as if my tongue was a paintbrush.
I never gave up,
Chef liked my dedication, determination.
He was getting older by the hour, as we all are,
but his old had started to bend his bones.
He was looking forward to more time off he said,
he thought I was ready, he said.
Ready for what? I said,
I'm not,
I'm definitely not . . .
what?!
It had been four years, me and him, happy.
Now here I was, my own kitchen to run.
Scary, yeh, but maybe one step away,
maybe a decade away from owning my own place.
Insane to think this could really happen!
It *was* happening to someone like me.
I mean, wow.

3

Chef *wipes the previous words off the whiteboard and writes
'Coconut Curried Tofu' on it.*

I miss the taste of coconut.
Scraping it from the shell
felt like hard work that then deserved
the melting of that wet white meat
between teeth and oh, I loved it.
We don't ever get coconut in here.
But this recipe is to keep dreams alive,
for those who will write it down, memorise.
Then when they get out, they'll cook it at home
for all of those that haven't abandoned them.
I decided to write this recipe book in here
to keep my creativity flowing,
even when faced with the grim ingredients provided.
I've carved out a little corner in this kitchen where I have –

She pauses.

Where I *did* have my own two trainees, Sasha and . . .
Candice. And I get – got a bit of freedom.
But no tofu or coconut.
I reckon with this book here I'm creating,
even just writing these recipes down,
well, it makes life taste better,
the air seems scented with possibility.
Or it did.

Today they asked me to cook egg fried rice,
something nice to keep you all calm on a day like this.
I nodded my head,
cos when they ask what they mean is
that's what you'll do,
regardless of what menu has been planned for weeks.
So I do. Or I will do. Soon.
They said I have to wait to find out . . .
Find out if I'm staying here or being moved,

being investigated, about what happened to –
Candice.
The egg fried rice. I'll do it soon.
I don't know what the fuck they reckon is calming
about egg fried rice though.
Grease and pieces of memories of plastic takeaway boxes
that most of these women got
with their boyfriends on weekends,
the end of the week that usually ended with an ending
that would end your faith in humanity –
like with my Annie, for example.
Every Friday after work she would pick up
boxes of gloop from the local Chinese,
breeze through the door all kisses
and stockings covering knees that were expected
to spend an unreasonable amount of time on the floor.
After he got what he needed the food would be left uneaten,
noodles gloomily looking through foggy containers
at a scene of all too common domestic distress,
chunks of sweet and sour chicken solidifying
under the soundwaves of unextraordinary anger
directed towards the one
that was supposed to be the one that's loved.
Unloved black bean sauce sighing into itself
as fists vibrate worktops
and walls and doors and air and floors
and finally flesh always flesh,
sometimes bone,
then fist and bone would moan together
and tears would fall
and tissues would become the litmus test of
how much do you really love –
I really love
I really do
I'm sorry you know I
you know I wouldn't do
it's just that
you know that

the way you
the way I –
and the night is packed away into a black bin bag,
tagged with a *Let's not talk of that again,*
tomorrow will be better and maybe
we should just get pizza.

4

Chef *wipes the previous title off the board and writes*
'Yellowtail sashimi (on shaved turnip with rhubarb gravy)'.

Sashimi was my favourite out there.
I used to shave a turnip,
cover a marinated slab of rose petal pink raw fish with it,
cushioned with juice from a rhubarb and oh my god,
it tasted like heaven.
I imagine it as I write it down.
I do a lot of that. Imagining.
I imagine my restaurant, when I get out.
It's going to be industrial chic. You know the type.
Exposed brick, bare lightbulbs
with unenvironmentally friendly
but unbelievably more beautiful glowing filaments.
Concrete floors,
waiting staff who take orders without notepads
and know everything there is to know about the menu
and the menu – oh!
There will be pickled cucumbers
compressed into octagonals,
origami pastrami pastry,
cod cheeks and celery,
exquisite mash with gravy
and soup that is never soup but always broth,
chilled broth –
like with avocado tomato and fig
because I really hate
the taste of hot liquid on my tongue.
The taste buds don't deserve to be burnt
and my memories of hot soup
aren't ones I want to pass on . . .

5

The first time I felt the heat of soup on my skin
I was working on a sailboat in the Shetland Islands.
Was the first time I'd been in charge of a kitchen, too.

My dad was an army man, an angry man,
definitely not much of a family man.
Moved to the lower arctic middle bit of fucking nowhere
to grow salmon in a farm and smoke it.
Then one summer out of nowhere he invites me
to sail the north seas with him.
Mum wasn't too keen on letting me go,
he'd left her with not much more than a reshaped nose
and scars that would make sure he was always around
even when he hadn't eaten a meal with us for five years.
But I was sixteen and far from sweet.
I wanted to piss her off and also to get off the estate,
go somewhere that spat superiority at the local park.
So I went up there with a backpack,
oilskins and rubber boots.
Things I'd never be seen dead wearing in my high street,
but on the high seas things were different,
leaving land, paint pot houses on a cloudy canvas.
Fog that looks so cosy setting in,
strong wind making my hair sing
as loud as shipping forecasts
in staccato Scottish harmonies.
I shivered to the sound of barnacled propellers
and the deep laughs of *don't tell 'er indoors*
that bobbed from bunk to deck
as they told jokes I didn't get
and put up posters of women they'd never met.

I used to just smile and stay on the side,
steer the boat sometimes, stare a lot.
I'd never been in love
but I decided that I'd know when I was
because the man would remind me of the way

seagulls glide out of stalactite clouds,
suddenly,
smoothly,
that's how he'd find me.
A kid's dreams.

My dad knew how I liked to cook,
always helping whoever was doing it,
adding my own ingredients,
making meals taste the way fresh air does
when your window's been closed all night
and the sweat has stuck to your duvet.
The crew felt free when they ate my food they said,
thought only of the present, bit like meditation,
not that we'd do that hippy shit,
but you get it, Chef, don't ya?
I did, kinda,
though I was too ecstatic at being called 'Chef'
to bother figuring out the metaphor.
Dad swore excitedly
and handed the kitchen galley over to me.
I thought I'd scored, he was doing me a first ever favour,
realising later it was the thing they all hated to do the most.
That day I cut veg as the boat swayed,
the edge of the blunt blade bit my thumb,
bit of blood on the onions,
no big deal,
blue plaster on,
carry on.
Served up thick, hot soup in cups, buttered bread.
Made my way up the stairs
only one cup,
one slice at a time.
Fine, swaying but okay.
Good balance from days spent on a skateboard as a kid.
Waves drip their blue beards over the deck,
I get up and down four times
and it's the last step up,

the cup in my hand,
the bread sitting on its rim,
the handle's heat softening my forefinger's cuticle.
Then Trident or Jupiter or Mars or Ares
lurches at the boat
with the fury of a Friday night closing time
after production line lay-offs
and off I went – over my ankle
trip
quick
flick of the toe
can't grip
slip slip slip
soup flicks
orange bits everywhere
hair stuck sticky steam –

You stupid dumb fuckin bitch what's wrong with you
can't even carry some stupid cups of fucking soup
fucking useless you int ya
little shit
I should throw you in that cunting sea
see see see
see what I can do to you
see what I mean
you stupid dumb –

he strangled and strangled me
until I couldn't breathe.
Like my neck was a winch
his fingers becoming the lengths of rope
that oxoxoxoxoed over and over again.
His eyes awash with waves
of his own dad's whisky skin,
until one bloke stepped forward
with a wet cloth,
Don't worry boss,
I'll mop that up.
Just like that Dad forgot

to keep doing those things to my skin
that made me remember
what it was like to have him as a live-in father.
I jumped off at the next harbour
and didn't cook again for five years.

6

Chef *wipes the previous title from the board and writes*
'Red wine risotto (with mushroom marmalade)'.

I try and find the ones in here
who have a knack with the food.
They come and train with me.
I'm strict, demanding, but fair, I think.
No shouting,
in a well-run kitchen there's no need for shouting.
No Gordon Ramsaying round here.
There's two main deputies after me.
Sasha, she deals with scrubbing the veg,
but her very best speciality is mushrooms.
She don't say much,
but she knows how to make amazing mushroom sauce
and she smiles a lot. I've got her back.
Then there is, there was,
Candice . . .
Good at mashing and with rolling pin things,
plus she sings sweeter than Manuka honey on iced mango
so I love to have her around.
When I'm feeling a little low a little slow,
her voice speeds me up,
makes me remember that it's good to be alive,
isn't it?
Even just a little bit,
even if sometimes it feels like
why would you want to be alive
when you're holed up here?
We met on my first day,
You ain't gonna last long with them books in ya arms,
she said.
I showed her pictures of food in the cookbooks I held
and her whole face changed,
became quiet and soft like misplaced compliments.
Later on, she told me when other inmates stole stock,
she lent me socks when mine had holes in,

she made me laugh when nobody came to see me.
Oh Candice . . .
Who sings sweeter than Manuka honey on iced mango.
You know, there's such a sad story behind the melodies,
I suppose there usually is.
When she was a kid her mum had an affair
with her dad's dad and so her dad
attacked his dad with an axe
until every bit of his cheating brains had been spat out,
then went round to his own house,
stuck a hose down his wife's throat
until she bloated so full of water she pretty much burst
and then he ran to the railway at the back of the garden,
flung himself onto the tracks in front of a cargo train
that didn't even stop as pieces of his flesh
spotted all the leaves on all the trees all around the tracks.
Candice . . .
Well she saw all of that.
Not the axe bit but the rest of it.
She was just a kid, nine or ten.
No mum or dad or granddad.
A grandma who tried her best but died
when Candice was fourteen, so she went to homes
and was one of many
who got groomed into becoming girls
who do things for boys
who will never be men.
It's a miracle really that she hadn't killed anybody,
she just got caught trying to steal a microwave from Currys
which when you think about what she's been through,
I mean who gives two tosses about a bloody microwave?
But this judge did for some reason,
maybe he was breathing rotten air that day
or had given up smoking or was trying to make a point
about stealing being wrong when you live in a place so right?
Who knows?
She came in here and tried to take her own life
in a whole host of imaginative ways.

Each time a quick stay in the medical ward,
another pop into the psych rooms,
which were full of women who were being marked down
as just having a 'strange turn'
because the officials didn't want
suicide attempts counted up by governments
who might take away budgets, bids, contracts even.
When I heard about it all, the lengths she went to,
I thought this girl needs some responsibility,
some purpose, so I had some words with the governor,
a man called Dave,
okay, give her a permanent kitchen position
but don't let her near the knives!
Sign here and here to prove I've said what I've said
and good luck, Chef.

I put her on mashing duty.
Taught her how to make
the best potatoes or turnip or celeriac,
or whatever other root I can convince them to provide,
at just the right consistency using only peelers, mashers
and if cutting was required she passed it on.
I was keeping my promise, my responsibility.
She seemed to like the sounds of the kitchen,
metallic rhythms mixed with her saccharine tones.
When she felt like letting loose
I would come in on the chorus
and Sasha would just nod along.
So we were cool in there,
we're alright, we're fine,
getting through our time one day at a time.
That's what I'd say to her and then –

She pauses.

They said they can't tell us anything.
Not even me.
It's like a huge secret.
I mean we saw her bleeding,

I stepped in her blood,
I was in her blood.
I mean she was just there right there,
I just asked how she was,
then she said all that . . . stuff.
I'd just said,
hey Candice how are you doing?
She turned on me and usually
I would never be there like that with it in my hand,
usually I'd never be near her with anything
she could use like that,
I signed I promised I knew –
but maybe I was thinking of something else
or maybe I wanted to test her . . .
No, no that's not what I wanted to do,
definitely not, she was, she is the best one here.
It's. Shit . . .
The way her wrist just flicked the knife from my hand
so dextrously, so delicately
until she – then it –
the bleeding was so deep I couldn't breathe.
She didn't speak it was so quick,
I screamed they came quick,
I flipped tea towels over the cut,
tripped on the blood,
it stuck to my apron to my nose to my shoes
and I swear she laughed.
I have a bruise now, a big bruise.
They took a picture, said they might need it for future,
for future evidence, in case there was a case,
in case I was involved somehow.
I'm like how,
how could I have been involved
she's my girl, she's my girl
I never did anything!
Yeh, yeh,
that's something we've never heard, Chef.
Don't worry yourself sure it will be fine,

she's unlikely to die, it looked deeper than it was.
This time you probably won't get the blame,
be a shame if you did, we know you liked that kid,
but you know how it goes.
It don't look great you got her blood on your nose
and the knives are locked up, it's only you with the key
and you signed you signed and Dave said
you know she's your responsibility
it's your responsibility –

7

Mum said I didn't have a good sense of responsibility.
That what happened was in one way or the other
because of me, I should just accept it.
She did.

Dad had a hard time of it in the salmon-farming business.
Even the fish thought he was a dick,
didn't want to be around him either.
First sniff of a sea change related infection
and they were like 'yeh, see you later',
took it on and dropped,
floated up to the top.
Let's remember
he was an army man, an angry man
definitely not much of a family man.
Mum said he had seen deaths undeserved
on the side of the road
and maybe he had killed.
I thought he had definitely killed.
His eyes had that capability to reflect
everything he was seeing so it never really had to go in,
defence mechanism for those who do things
beyond vision, beyond retelling.
Imagine something so bad it could never be retold,
that's the look his whole being owned.
I always hoped he hadn't passed it on to me.

The fish died.
I never got to ask him,
but I guess that made him think about his own death,
the blood and guts mess he'd made of his life.
So he came to London, to find me, my mum,
apologise, start a new life with new lies.

I was closing up, mid-week quiet night.
There was mud on his boots,
it hadn't rained for a while.
He stood there
like he should be there,

as if he could never be unwelcome.
There wasn't one bit of his bobbled skin
that I wanted to let in,
this was my kitchen,
my fucking kitchen,
his boots his mud his muck wasn't welcome.
Come in, he said,
can I come in?
I ignored him.
It was late,
I was cleaning,
scrubbing silver to lake-lit moonlight,
the last night before the first night off in ten days.
Swaying with tiredness,
the tonelessness of his voice
fighting with the memory I had of its bite.
What for,
what do you wanna come in for?
I didn't even look up,
kept scrubbing,
wiping.
See,
I want to see you.
I'm here, you've seen.
What do you want from me?
Nothing, I want nothing.
You should leave.
I need you to see me.
I won't look.
Wiping still, I wonder if my cooking
will be spoilt by this intrusion,
will this memory infuse all my soft fruits,
plait itself into my pastry?
Just leave me and my kitchen.
I let you run your first one.
Bullshit.
On the ship, I did.
Yeh, then you tried to twist all the breath outta me,
leave me be.

I'm not giving in.
Go. You're too slow.
It's all over, no daughter for you.
If you don't let me,
I mean it's all that's keeping me going really,
it's all I want, it's all I –
don't give a shit.

Now I look.
He's got broken eyes
and a starry heart stuck in thunderclouds.
The sight makes my soul quiet but my voice loud
and I shout.
Now you ain't proud?
You wanna come to love me,
come to get loved by me?
See where I am? Do you see?
There will be a Michelin star on this window.
I cook here, create here,
make here be as much of life as I can
because outside of this
I'm not safe,
I don't know the way.
Your way was where you went
and there wasn't any space there for me.
You bring flesh and blood to air
and expect it to what?
Live without love for so long that it moulds its own,
saving all that for the day you decide to come back?
My life has been made up of days waiting
to discover darker parts of myself.
Digging inside skin until I can pull out
exactly what is so bad about me that makes everyone leave,
believing that those parts are the markings
that map the outlines of my life,
of who I can be
and so of course off I go to find those
that stretch that, scratch that

tell me to forget that,
those thoughts are of no importance
based in no truth whatsoever –
but then do you know what they do?
Of course you do cos it's what you did,
what you do.
Everyone fucking leaves.
So I will not mend your broken eyes
with stitches of moisture
from my soaked-through scrapbook.
No, no, that's not me,
that's not who you made.
This is the last thing I'll ever say to you,
please, Dad, just fucking leave.

And he did.
And there was that sinking part of me
that wanted him to refuse,
to use his helicopter voice,
cut through the density of pre-dawn London
and tell me no,
I will stay here until you let me speak with you,
about things that those who come
from someone's insides should probably at least try out.
Like, what TV shows do you watch?
Do you get to go out much? Did you study?
Who broke your heart? Did you cry?
What song do you want played when you've died?

But there was none of that.
Just the back of an old man,
leaving one last time.

A few months later I was round Mum's for Sunday dinner.
She liked to cook for me in front of her friends,
so she could say,
See, even the famous local chef can't say no to my roasties!
And it's true, they were the best,
I always took my own gravy though.

When everyone had left that day she told me,
Your dad's dying you know,
he's not got long.
Oh.
I don't want to talk about –
Everyone deserves a bit of forgiveness.
He got a bit.

Two years went past.
The phone rang,
he was raspy on the other end, no anger now,
quiet.
I can't leave the flat anymore.
I've got you on speakerphone because I can't hold it anymore.
At night time when there's no carer,
I get stuck in the toilet and I sleep there,
in my shit, bathroom floor cool on my skin.
They will take me to a home soon,
I've never had a home, I won't go.
He had not one person in the world,
he wanted to pass away,
stop being a burden to himself,
to the memories of everyone else.
He knew it was a lot to ask,
but he thought I might enjoy it,
do us both the biggest favour.
He had it all figured out,
he wanted me to inject a lethal dose of something into him
so it worked quicker, nicer.
He'd be gone so quick, so nice.
I said, how can I do that, Dad?
The phone dropped, went dead.
I went round, picked it up for him.
Against my better judgement yes,
but when I saw him so helpless
I felt –

* (This memory of the past is now interspersed with more recent
questioning about Candice.

*As the scene progresses, in amongst reliving the court trial she faced
for her dad's murder, in which she was found guilty, she is also faced
with the questioning from prison officials over Candice's apparent
suicide.)*

Glad,
maybe you were glad when Candice asked you for help,
like your dad did?
Maybe this is it, you've found your calling,
helping people who want to die, die.
Although you can never prove they wanted to, can you?
No, no my calling is cooking.
Take a look at my CV it's clear for whoever wishes to see.
What exactly did she say to you?
She said,
the grey here creates a never-ending hurricane of dust
inside her mind.
I want to find the sea.
Will you help me?
I just said, 'How you doing, Candice?'
And that's what she said, she asked me to help her.
To find the sea?
Metaphorically.
You knew what she meant?
I knew what she meant, yes.
She was looking for death to lap up
the inconsequence of this existence.
She had tried so many times,
always got it wrong, got everything wrong.
You're the closest thing I've ever had to a friend, Chef.
She wanted me to help her go,
like she said she knew I'd done with him.
I said 'no, no, no'.
I would never do that,
I had never done that with him, they were wrong,
she was wrong, I had never done that. I –

Of course the fingerprints were mine,
it was my knife,

my kitchen,
it was in my hand,
she took it,
I'm telling you she took it,
have a look at her history,
her history isn't pretty,
she wanted to die.
She did.

* He did,
what's it got to do with me?
He wanted to die.
Check his history,
his history ain't pretty.
Domestic violence, PTSD
Iraq, fish farms,
rings all the alarms.
Do you accept that you didn't like your father much?
We accept that he didn't appear to like you.
Beat you, left you,
one time it looks like you almost died.
Can't have been nice, can it?
Can it?
We, the prosecution, put forward that revenge is a clear motive.
The defendant wanted her father dead,
using his disability
as a cover-up for her premeditated murder –
Objection!
Do you care at all what I have to say?
It wasn't me.
He wanted to die cos he lived a crap life.
He was a terrible example of a man and yes,
he's dead. Yes, I wanted him out of my life
but that doesn't mean I needed him to die.
Well we, and we venture the jury too,
wholeheartedly disagree.
Goodbye.

8

Chef *wipes the previous title off the board and writes*
'Red berries with hibiscus jasmine sorbet'.

It can be messy this one.
Red berries.
They're very soft,
leave trails of their sweet insides on the plate
if you don't treat them delicately enough.
They're everyone's favourite,
even when they're not real,
'Give me the red one pleeease!'
We used to shout for fruit gums, Opal Fruits,
whatever, those things with no fruit in them whatsoever.
The sorbet is difficult but delicious.
I wouldn't say it's for the amateurs,
but I'm hoping
that those who get to this point in the book
have a certain amount of skill
and most importantly determination.
For the sorbet, you will need eggs, caster sugar,
jasmine tea leaves and hibiscus flowers –
fresh, if possible.
Candice said her favourite drink was hibiscus tea.
Strange as she struck me as a PG Tips girl,
but you can never tell really, can you?

She died, they said.
Fatal penetrating injury to the lower left quadrant of the chest,
suggesting she aimed for the heart.
She missed, she always did.
The knife perforated the lower lobe of her left lung,
causing traumatic internal bleeding.
She must have grabbed your hand extremely hard
for the angle to remain at a lateral aspect
but we guess she was determined.
And between you and me,
we would far rather deal with a suicide fine

than get marked down with murder in the annual report,
nobody wants that, do they?

She would have loved a little sorbet
flavoured with her favourite tea flower.
Doesn't taste too sweet too soapy, just right for sorbet.
Just right for summer days.

When you put the berries on the plate
use a clean spoon for each one,
be gentle,
their red insides,
so sweet.
Don't let them creep onto the plate.
It's up to whoever eats the dish to decide
if the berries go inside the sorbet
or stay divided –
give them the choice.
There should always be a choice,
shouldn't there?

Battleface

The Bush Theatre was closed for its amazing refurbishment in 2016 and so took new work to the surrounding area, with short plays happening in schools, churches, nightclubs and hotels. *Battleface* was written before we knew what location was available and it ended up in the local school hall – which, though far from the facial rejuvenation specialist clinic I'd imagined, worked well in the end as it was set up as a kind of competitive sporting event. I'd been really interested in the cosmeticisation of botulinum, as botox, in particular its use in Iraq, a country militarily devastated by US and UK forces on the false pretext of stockpiling the very same chemical as a 'Weapon of Mass Destruction'. This was the first piece in which I started to explore writing about the world I had once worked in, at the Ministry of Defence.

Battleface opened at St Stephen's C of E Primary School, London, in September 2016, with the following cast and creative team:

Ablah	Agni Scott
Camilla	Jeany Spark
Director	Joe Murphy
Casting	Priscilla John Casting LTD

Camilla (*a journalist*) *and* **Ablah** (*a cosmetic doctor specialising in facial rejuvenation*) *are having an interview chat in a spare room at* **Ablah***'s clinic.*

Ablah   I'd estimate you're thirty-three years old, from the depth of the fountain of lines between your eyebrows. You take your job extremely seriously, working until the light late hours – revealed by the shade of dark skin under your eyes. You haven't been joyously happy for a while – the laughter lines around your mouth don't match your age. You don't eat well. You drink too much coffee. It gives you palpitations, but you drink it anyway because – because of this dedication to your work. And there's something else, something I can't quite put my finger on.

You'd have to sit under my lamp for a proper analysis.

Camilla   Wow. That was – amazing. I feel . . . naked.

Ablah   Accurate, then?

Camilla   I had no idea all that was right here, on my face.

Ablah   Most don't.

Camilla   So you really are the best.

Ablah   Well, no – maybe, one of.

Camilla   Why do you do what you do, Ablah?

Ablah   I love it.

Camilla   What exactly do you love about it?

Ablah   The possibility.

Camilla   Possibility?

Ablah   When a client comes to see me, they're hoping to rediscover their possibility. It's a beautiful thing to be able to help them do that.

Camilla   How *do* you do that?

Ablah   I allow time to be pulled back inside a person's being.

Camilla   Quite a feat.

Ablah   When they look in the mirror, they no longer see trauma, or disappointment, just –

Camilla   Possibility?

Ablah   Exactly.

Camilla   So, in a way, medical facial rejuvenation is like . . . therapy?

Ablah   Yes, except cheaper, faster and far more effective. Trust me on that.

Camilla   I will.

Ablah   And how about you, Camilla, why did you become a journalist?

Camilla   To meet the most interesting minds I possibly could without having one myself.

Ablah   An unfair assessment, I'm sure. I always felt the world could be changed with words.

Camilla   Do you write?

Ablah   I did. Years ago. Just . . . silly things, really.

Camilla   Like what?

Ablah   Poetry, mainly. I was an angry young woman!

Camilla   What were you angry about?

Ablah   The world being so far from what I wanted it to be.

Camilla   What did you want it to be?

Ablah   It was just . . . the usual stuff you feel before reality and responsibility take over.

Camilla   No poetry anymore then?

Ablah   No time for that, probably quite fortunately.

Camilla   Do you find time to do anything outside of work?

Ablah   Hardly, it's non-stop these days.

Camilla   I suppose the Best Botox Award helped with that?

Ablah   Maybe, but demand for these procedures has been increasing steadily for a long time.

Camilla   Why do you think that is?

Ablah   Hope. Despair. People need to be in control of something. Plain old vanity. So many reasons.

Camilla   Do you miss cardiology?

Ablah   Um. Well. I haven't asked myself that question for a long time.

Camilla   Perhaps that means no, then?

Ablah   Actually, I probably do. The urgency of it, the absolute life or death of it – that, maybe I miss that.

Camilla   I imagine it must be quite something, to save a life?

Ablah   There's nothing else that even comes close.

Camilla   So why did you leave?

Ablah   It was hard, as a single parent. The night shifts, the emergencies. Cosmetics was more manageable, back then.

Camilla   And more lucrative I bet?

Ablah   That side was appreciated too, but it took a long while to get this clinic to where it is today.

Camilla   What about your family now?

Ablah   What about them?

Camilla   Do you get to spend time with them?

Ablah   Not . . . as much as I'd like.

Camilla   Are they proud of the reputation you've achieved?

Ablah   I hope so. Sorry, how much longer do you –

Camilla   Not long, I know you're busy. I really appreciate your time.

Ablah   No problem.

Camilla   You said you have children?

Ablah   I have a son.

Pause.

Camilla   Nasim.

Ablah   Yes, Nasim. How do you – how do you know that?

Camilla   I met him.

Ablah   You met him? Where?

Camilla   At a party.

Ablah   But how did you know – how did you make the connection –

Camilla   He told me all about his famous botox doctor mother from Shepherd's Bush, it had to be you.

Ablah   He told you about me?

Camilla   You sound surprised.

Ablah   I – we . . . we've had a . . .

Camilla   He mentioned things have been a bit difficult.

Ablah   To say the least.

Camilla   He also said things are looking up, between you.

Ablah   You had quite an in-depth chat for a party, then?

Camilla   It was a Ministry party, for those who'd served in Iraq.

Pause. **Ablah** *takes this in.*

Ablah   And what would a journalist for a high-end lifestyle magazine be doing at such a party?

Pause. This is the opening for **Camilla** *to reveal herself. Change of tone, etc.*

Camilla   Ablah, the reason I need to speak to you today is far more important than to write a feature / on you –

Ablah   You're not writing a feature on me?

Camilla   No, I'm not.

Pause.

Ablah   What exactly are we doing here, then?

Camilla   We need to discuss something very important with you.

Ablah   'We'? I can only see you here, Camilla. What is this, what do you want?

Camilla   World peace and national security.

Ablah   How sweet.

Camilla   I'm serious, Ablah.

Ablah   You're not a journalist.

Camilla   No.

Ablah   Who are you?

Camilla   You'll always know me as Camilla.

Ablah   I really dislike games. At school, I used to pretend I had my period every single week in order to avoid playing any kind of game.

Camilla   Funny. PE was my favourite subject. Always thought I'd grow up to be a runner.

Look I apologise for the underhand method to get you talking to me. We just find it's easier than an unexpected knock at the door.

Ablah   'We', who is this 'we'?

Camilla   We need you, Ablah. We need your talent and we need your insight, nobody else will do.

Ablah   Again, oh my, I'm not understanding exactly who 'we' is?

Camilla   I work for a section, a special section, of the Ministry.

Ablah   The Ministry as in *the* Ministry?

Camilla   We've been searching for someone who fits your profile for a while now.

Ablah   *My* profile? The Ministry? I / mean –

Camilla   When Nasim mentioned / you I –

Ablah   Just hold. The hell. Up. I don't even know where to begin / with –

Camilla   I understand it's a bit of a shock, but your cooperation is paramount / to –

Ablah   Shock? I thought I was spending my lunch hour being interviewed by *Gun Magazine* for God's sake and now it's – I don't know, what is this?

Camilla   As I was saying, when Nasim mentioned you I –

Ablah   That, that there, I just – When you say Nasim mentioned me, do you mean he just mentioned me, as in passing conversational mentioned, or do you mean mentioned me as in . . .

Camilla   Conversational only. He doesn't know about this meeting.

Ablah   What – why was he even *at* a Ministry party? He didn't 'serve' in Iraq, he was a bloody mercenary.

Camilla   We couldn't survive without them these days, Ablah, although nobody says mercenary anymore, it's private security mostly.

Ablah   Oh well, in that case –

Camilla   The best of them become, well, good friends with the Ministry.

Ablah   Nasim has left all that behind now.

Camilla   I'm here to talk about you –

Ablah   So what – what the hell is this 'profile' of mine exactly?

Camilla   I'm going to give you as much information as I can.

Ablah   That would be appreciated, information, that would be good.

Camilla   Do you want some water?

Ablah   This is my bloody office! If I want some water I'll get some water.

Camilla   Of course.

Ablah   I'm not even sure why you're still in here, actually. I should just ask you to leave.

Camilla   I'm sure you'd like to know what I have to say.

Ablah   *I'm* sure that whatever you say will be a load of bullshit.

Camilla   Look, I completely understand your slight hostility to the Ministry, perhaps even to this country, but / what we –

Ablah   Ha, *slight* hostility? Surely, in a 'special section' you do your research before you ambush someone?

Camilla   You don't have Facebook.

Ablah   Are you serious?

Camilla   These days it's tricky when someone has no personal online presence.

Ablah   World-class intelligence.

Camilla   All we could find was an article written when you were a student, arguing the Palestinian case against Israeli expansionism.

Ablah   And from that you couldn't surmise how I'd feel about being approached by a government that still supports such actions all these decades later?

Camilla   You're a famous cosmetic doctor specialising in facial rejuvenation. It doesn't scream socialist. Getting older makes us see things differently.

Ablah   Not things like apartheid and occupation, Camilla.

Camilla   What we need you for is so significant to our strategy, Ablah, we are willing to overlook any ideological differences. I hope that gives you an indication of how important this is?

Ablah *settles a little. Feels more in control again now. Looks at her watch.*

Ablah   Well, you better get on with it then, my PA will be welcoming my next clients soon.

Camilla   Have you heard of the upward trend in cosmetic facial treatments in Iraq, particularly in Baghdad?

Ablah   I'm aware.

Camilla   The relative rate of treatments is outnumbering those even in America.

Ablah   And?

Camilla   Every woman who can afford it – and a few men – are botoxing and peeling and nose-jobbing their way out of decades of despair.

Ablah   Poetic, your point?

Camilla   You said yourself, what you do is better than therapy.

Ablah   I believe so.

Camilla   Your fellow Iraqis (**Ablah** *rolls her eyes at this phrasing*) obviously agree, there's only four registered psychiatrists in Baghdad – *but* 344 people are licensed to administer botox.

Ablah   A licence doesn't mean they have a clue what they're doing.

Camilla   Exactly!

She is excited that **Ablah** *has said this.* **Ablah** *scrutinises her.*

Ablah   Oh God, do you want me – no, you/ can't be –

Camilla   We want you to run a clinic, just like this one, but in Baghdad.

Ablah   I don't want to run a clinic in Baghdad.

Camilla   You'll be in stratospheric demand – the best botox doctor in London *and* she's Iraqi, perfect.

Ablah   Again. Slowly. I – don't – want – to – run a clinic – in Baghdad. I'm very happy in Shepherd's Bush, thank you.

Camilla   As you know, clients talk when they have treatments. They're nervous, it's intimate, they *talk*. ISIS have a stronghold there, in Iraq, and we –

Ablah   Camilla, I get it. You want me to *spy* for you? For Her Majesty's Government?

Camilla   We want you to provide the unrivalled service and skills you do here, whilst encouraging those who come to see you to . . . let you in to their personal lives a little.

Ablah   Their personal lives . . . and details of planned suicide attacks they might just blurt out in the middle of me injecting their epidermis?

Camilla   Nobody else can do this.

Ablah   How do you know?

Camilla   We run a training centre out there. 200 students per year. The best teachers. And still, not / one –

Ablah   A training centre for spies who can do botox?

Camilla   A training centre for cosmetic surgery and aesthetic treatments.

Ablah   An official cosmetic surgery training centre run by British intelligence in Iraq?

Camilla   It's run by a quango, of course, there's no official link to intelligence at all, but it's no secret that the UK Government support it.

Ablah   I've never heard of it.

Camilla   Cosmetic surgery is an important industry in a post-conflict locality.

Ablah   *Post*-conflict?

Camilla   Well, officially. Look, we encourage anything that subverts the political rhetoric and the idea that women should cover themselves. We want them to feel free.

Ablah   Whilst spying on them?

Camilla   We only want to know more about certain women, not average citizens.

Ablah   What you've said, you know, it shows how nothing's changed.

Camilla   Meaning?

Ablah   The level of knowledge you have of Iraqi life, after all this time. It's still superficial and insufficient. Women can get their noses hacked away and their faces frozen to the ice age but they'll stay covered and if they don't, that doesn't make them more free – you must know that?

Camilla   We don't have the data.

Ablah   God, you don't need data, Camilla, you just need eyes.

Camilla   We need your eyes.

Ablah, *exhausted, needs to put this to bed.*

Ablah   Have you read the Chilcot Report?

Camilla   An abridged version, yes.

Ablah   Don't you feel ashamed?

Camilla   I was very junior at that time. And, I believe our advice wasn't listened to, intelligence agencies weren't to blame.

Ablah   So what's the point?

Camilla   Of?

Ablah   Of what you do, of what you're asking me to do, if nobody listens when it matters anyway?

Camilla   Many of the top minds behind ISIS are female. Wives of the cabinet being our main interest area at the moment.

Ablah   And miraculously, out of the 345 ones available, they'll go to see a botox doctor newly arrived from London?

Camilla   They have to maintain a high status within their groups and a high status as a woman is impossible to maintain without a ferocious approach to anti-ageing, as you'll know. They will want the best.

Ablah   It is funny.

Camilla   What?

Ablah   I've wanted to be in a room with one of you people for so long and now here I am and I can't even catch my thoughts –

Camilla   We're conscious of the fact we've made plenty of mistakes when it comes to / Iraq –

Ablah   Mistakes?!

Camilla   That's why we're pursuing non-traditional routes into finding out what we can about those intent on destroying innocent lives.

Ablah   Innocent lives. I wonder what you mean by innocent.

Camilla   I mean people who aren't planning to attack other people.

Ablah   Do you know anyone who died there?

Camilla   Yes. My partner. She was twenty-three.

Ablah   I am sorry to hear that. Truly.

Camilla   The company who made the armour for the vehicle she was in made some redundancies to save costs. They didn't realise they'd got rid of everyone who knew how to fit the armour.

Ablah   And yet, you carried on?

Camilla   Ablah, I can't stand here and give you a speech on the magnificence of the monarchy and the righteousness of our military interventions. I know plenty of them, but – that's not why I do this.

Ablah   You believe you can make a difference? Save some lives?

Camilla   I know I can, I do. The work we do, it saves lives, it keeps at least some people safe, we just can't make a poster out of it.

Ablah   I arrived here when I was fifteen. We literally walked through flames to find ourselves here, in Shepherd's

Bush. It wasn't as friendly then as it is now, not as easy to find a piece of home. My mother didn't speak anymore. She'd refused to leave Iraq earlier. My sister and my brother, younger than me, twelve and ten. Small, sweet faces, big eyes. They were the cherished ones. I was arrogant, precocious, rebellious. The two little ones were cheeky but adoring of my parents. They loved doing anything for them. In Iraq, one day, they went out to the market for my mother, she'd ran out of the cheese my father lived for. I was sulking, listening to music, doodling the name of a boy I had a crush on all over my schoolbooks. Life continues as much as it can, even when it has been deemed worthless by those in buildings like the one where you work.

We all heard the explosion. So quick. Like a pillowcase being ripped in half whilst you sleep on it. Then the falling. A sprinkling, really. Bricks and limbs and pipes and poles falling so softly, like raindrops from where we stood, searching with our eyes. We couldn't see the damage, only hear it. We stood frozen outside the house, me, my mother and father, wishing our ears to be wrong, wishing to see their small, sweet faces running to us, laughing that they'd played a trick, they'd made us think we were in a film, here is the cheese, baba, here is a kiss, ammi, here is a hug, big sister.

We had to wrap parts of their little bodies together in a white cloth because we didn't know who was who.

My father said we had to go then, at least to save me, the uncherished child who was now the only child and so cherished, a little. My mother didn't argue because she didn't speak. We made our awkward, painful, silent way here, to you, and I was glad, I really was. I flourished.

Camilla   What about your mother?

Ablah   To lose children, there's no coming back from that.

Camilla   It must be . . . horrific.

Ablah   So many children have died in Iraq. All over. So many, still dying. Small bodies, the cloth for five of them can be made from one adult's shroud. If they can even be found, to be buried. War, Camilla, does not keep any people 'safe'.

Pause. **Ablah** *upset.* **Camilla** *is momentarily saddened by this accusation of failure on her part.*

Camilla   I know we're asking a lot from you, Ablah, and we wouldn't do so / unless –

Ablah   Did Nasim tell you why we've had a difficult relationship?

Camilla   No, he didn't.

Ablah   I hadn't spoken to him for five years until two months ago.

Camilla   Five years is a long time.

Ablah   To not speak to your only child? It's a lifetime.

Camilla   Because he went to Iraq?

Ablah   Despite all my stories, all my ranting to him against the war machine, despite never having heard a 'hello' from his grandma, never being able to meet his uncle and aunty, he still decided the money was too good to say no to. To privately patrol a prison camp. For the British Army. Unthinkable. Indigestible. I – well, everything is a failure after that.

Camilla   He came back safe.

Ablah   Thank God, *he* did. Who knows what happened to those he patrolled . . . But now that I'm talking to him again, trying, trying to untangle how we could hold such opposing views on such fundamental matters, squeezing out the love in my heart to cover the scars of sorrow he caused me – I simply cannot step away from him to do what you're asking me to, even if I wanted to. Do you understand, Camilla? I won't leave my son again.

Pause.

Camilla   I had hoped to tell you this once you'd agreed, as a pleasant surprise of sorts. I hadn't anticipated / such –

Ablah   What, tell me what?

Camilla   Nasim is . . . He's working for us now.

Ablah   No. No.

Camilla   He's been through the recruitment process, all the vetting, the training.

Ablah   You fucking . . . you stood there and knew . . . he told me he was working on writing, he was going on a . . . course –

Camilla   He's legally obliged to not reveal where he works, of course.

Ablah   What is he going to be doing –

Camilla   I can't tell you –

Ablah   Bullshit you've just told me more than you should anyway. So tell me.

Camilla   He . . . he's due to be deployed to Baghdad, soon.

Pause.

Ablah   For how long?

Camilla   Two months, to begin with.

Ablah   To begin with?

Camilla   He has a lot of talent, very promising.

Ablah   You vultures!

Camilla   Ablah –

Ablah   How can you do this to people? You know what it feels like to lose someone senselessly, or was that all just a lie to get me talking –

Camilla   That was the truth.

Ablah   And yet – and yet – are you even human?

Camilla   This is what I can do. To make the world I want to see.

Ablah   Why did you tell me about Nasim?

Camilla   I was always planning to. I just thought it would be under . . . more favourable circumstances.

Ablah   Are you able to stop his deployment? Do you have that authority?

Camilla   I can't stop him being deployed. I could certainly cite conflict of interests – if you were going to be there, of course – and push that he's sent elsewhere or given a London-based desk job for a while.

Ablah   Desk job. You must give him a desk job.

Camilla   I can only do that if the conflict of interest is there – you.

Ablah   If I say yes, when will I become . . . active?

Camilla   Next week, ideally. We have the clinic ready, the timing is crucial, for reasons I can't tell you yet, until you sign.

Ablah   Will he know?

Camilla   He's still junior. He won't be cleared to that level. We'll come up with a reason.

Ablah   Would you be able to guarantee he would never be deployed to Iraq?

Camilla   For as long as I'm employed by the Ministry, yes. Beyond that, no.

Pause.

I'm aware you need to get back to work soon.

Ablah   Yes.

Camilla   But this is quite urgent, due to the –

Ablah   Crucial timing?

Camilla   Yes.

Ablah   If I say no?

Camilla   We really hope you won't.

Ablah   If I do?

Camilla   Nasim will go to Baghdad . . .

Ablah   And?

Camilla   And counter-terrorism measures have become pretty comprehensive these days.

Ablah   You'd arrest me?

Camilla   We could.

Ablah   Would you? Really?

Camilla   There's been a lot of arrests. For women with . . . your background.

Ablah   I take it you don't mean in medicine.

Camilla   The first person to be convicted under the updated anti-terrorism legislation was a Muslim woman who wrote poetry.

Ablah   Poetry?

Camilla   About decapitation and various, worryingly violent things.

Ablah   Ever read *American Psycho*? Bret Easton Ellis?

Camilla   I'm not saying I agree, I'm saying it's not as difficult as you may think.

Ablah   If you look like me, you mean? So the 'terror poet' has been taken. Would I be the 'botox bomber'?

Camilla   Who knows what would happen, but the slightest incident wouldn't be good for business, would it?

Ablah   You'd be surprised, Camilla, not everybody shares your love of queen and country.

Camilla   It must have been difficult, growing up.

Ablah   How do you mean?

Camilla   In a country you're not from. Viewed with hatred at worst, pity at best. Unspoken suspicion of deserving your fate following you around.

Ablah   I told you, I flourished here.

Camilla   You had to, you're a survivor. But they didn't make it easy, did they?

Ablah   Nothing in life is easy.

Camilla   At school, being the refugee kid, the one nobody wanted to sit next to, the one nobody spoke to, the one who had to learn the language quick enough to pass tests all the other kids had been preparing for since they were born. The one nobody chose for their team at PE – is that why you hated it so much?

Ablah   This is beneath even you.

Camilla   Proving your worth, proving you could do it, do anything you wanted, do better than they all could – that's what got you out of bed every day. That's what gave you the strength to look at your silent mother and tell her about your day as if she'd asked.

Ablah   Stop it.

Camilla   Nobody to believe in you, everyone to expect nothing from you. The reserves of belief you must have buried inside you, Ablah, it's incredible.

Ablah   You do not know me.

Camilla   Every step you made you had to justify why you were allowed to take it before you could make the next one.

You had to laugh at jokes that broke your heart at first until you got so used to it, you started making them yourself.

Ablah   I'm not sure I've made who I am clear enough –

Camilla   You had to be validated at every stage by someone else – a man, someone who'd already made it, someone trusted, someone British, someone white. From school to college to uni to hospitals to clinics –

Ablah   What is your point, Camilla, just shut up and tell me! What is your goddamn point?!

Camilla   I could make it all unhappen, Ablah. All that work. A lifetime of work. Of sacrifice, of soul-destroying boundary bending. A high-profile arrest. Rumours. Association with unfavourables from back home. It would be so easy for us, so utterly, boringly easy that it makes me feel nauseous, to be honest. Because I admire you and I would hate to have to do that to someone of your conviction and strength.

Ablah *is very upset – this is unbearable.*

Ablah   But you would.

Camilla   I would.

Ablah   Your dedication is exemplary.

Camilla   You have a real opportunity here, Ablah.

Ablah   Yes, perhaps I do.

Camilla   Okay?

She is searching for her answer. **Ablah** *takes her time.*

Ablah   Do you know that botulinum is the most toxic chemical in the world to humans? That botox is a form of that, the very thing people pay to have injected into their faces?

Camilla Yes, I'm aware. It's also one of the chemicals Saddam was suspected of stockpiling for biological warfare.

Ablah All those Iraqi women, hoping to find love, acceptance, some tingle of excitement again, something, anything, all with the help of the very thing that was used to justify the decimation of their lives, and the cosmetic use of it was invented by the country that orchestrated all that destruction. Irony doesn't begin to cover it.

Camilla It is what it is.

Ablah Did you choose Nasim for his role, just so you could get me?

Camilla No. He applied a long time ago. It was just lucky that he mentioned what you did.

Ablah Lucky for who?

Camilla Like I said, this is an opportunity for someone of your . . . passion.

Pause. Is **Camilla** *encouraging* **Ablah** *to cause trouble?*

Ablah *is really struggling with what to do.*

Camilla *checks her phone/watch.*

Camilla Ablah?

Ablah I know how to kill.

Camilla There won't be any killing.

Ablah There's always killing.

Camilla Not for you.

Ablah For the drones? For Nasim?

Camilla This is about saving lives, not taking them, isn't it?

She is almost looking for **Ablah**'s *validation on this point.*

Ablah If I was to open a tiny, undiluted bottle of botulinum
– which is luckily very easy for someone like me to come by –

and put it here, between us, the airborne particles from this deadly toxin would likely kill us both relatively quickly, perhaps before my PA, sitting just out there, came knocking. I wonder though, if one of us had significant exposure to botox already, they might outlive the other long enough to get help for themselves, just in time.

Camilla   But you don't have that tiny bottle, do you, Ablah?

Ablah   It's all about possibility, isn't it, Camilla?

Blackout.

the love i feel is red

This play was written for the same wonderful daytime theatre project as *Clean* – A Play, a Pie and a Pint – commissioned by Oran Mor in Glasgow and the Tobacco Factory Theatre in Bristol. I really wanted to explore an intergenerational dynamic on stage, as my characters so far had all been under fortyish. I also wanted to explore different themes of loss and grief and the many taboos that still remain in women's lives today, no matter their age. Reflecting back, it's an extreme context in which to explore a nuanced look at one woman's experience of abortion and another woman's experience of miscarriage, but I wanted to try and create different threads of grief and grieving, something British society has not developed cultural mechanisms for dealing with, to me.

I do hope there is absolutely no doubt throughout that I would never endorse any arguments against abortion, but I also wish to challenge the homogenisation of responses to having one from *some* of those who campaign for pro-choice. I understand why that can occur, because any chink of regret or suffering can be used by the anti-abortionists to try and add weight to their misogynistic thinking. However, those who have had an abortion must also be able to express whatever range of emotions and experiences resulted from that choice without fear of being labelled as someone giving fuel to the fascist fire and find solidarity and support in admitting that they maybe did not feel okay and it was not an easy process, yet it was still the one they would choose again – or not.

the love i feel is red opened at the Tobacco Factory, Bristol, as part of the A Play, a Pie and a Pint season in May 2016, with the following cast and creative team:

Mona	Janet Etuk
Susan	Heather Williams
Director	Nel Crouch
Designer	Rebecca Jane Wood
Lighting Designer	Joe Price
Producer	Jojo Townsend

1

We see **Susan** *(fifties) in a living room, in a house.*

Susan   I never agreed with armbands. For a number of reasons, not least the fizzing fluorescence of them, like birds wearing high-vis jackets amongst rainforest foliage – it just seems a little, well, unnecessary. There were a few dark blue ones I didn't find so affronting. The ones with cartoon characters were probably the worst – cartoon characters seem to get bloody everywhere, don't they? Such an assault to eyes accustomed to the pickled blue of a clean, chlorinated swimming pool.

I also found fault with the apparent purpose of armbands. Filled as they are with somebody else's breath – often mine, if a rushed parent hadn't poked the . . . the rubbery nozzle thing in properly. Another's breath, it always seemed to me, is an entirely unsatisfactory way to keep afloat.

If a child started in my class with armbands, which many of them did, I would ask them what they were most scared about – water-wise – and from there we would have a considered discussion about fear. Once we'd done this, most of the children would realise they weren't as afraid as they thought and *were* willing to have a go at assisted swimming without armbands. Children are far more progressive at letting go of fear than adults I always found. Once they'd had some help, it was about gently coaxing them into embracing the water with just the aid of their own limbs. And the satisfaction of that, empowering a child to release their body to the water and enjoy it, well, I'm not sure I'll ever find something quite like that again.

Ty was the only one who refused to do things my way, in the swimming pool or elsewhere, I suppose. I had a five-point plan that I never thought too early to share with the children, but Ty used to laugh at it, even before he could properly speak. He used to mimic me.

'Buoyancy. Coordination. Health. Fitness. Water safety.'

Buoyancy. Coordination. Health. Fitness. Water safety . . .

We now see **Mona** *(twenties) on stage, outside a front door. There is a cactus plant in a pot. Her first words overlap with the last line of* **Susan**'s.

Mona   Be safe. Train. Check. Have fun. Explore.

'Be safe. Train. Check. Have fun. Explore.'

Those were his rules. Ty's five-point plan that he used to try and teach me. I was like, babes, I was doing this before you even knew what kneepads were, but he always thought he knew better than everyone, wanted to teach even the people who taught him.

And you know, to be fair to him, he was sick at teaching, like kids loved him and he really brought out that enthusiasm you need if anyone's gonna take what you're teaching seriously. But there's no mystery about where he got that whole 'five-point plan, drill it in your brain until you sweat it out between your legs' business is there? His mum, classic control freak.

The first time we met, me and Ty, we were on a window ledge at some abandoned warehouse everyone was using to try out their moves and I couldn't stop staring at his nose. It was big. That's not a bad thing. I don't know why that's seen here like a bad thing. I love big noses. Very . . . authoritative. If someone with a small nose told me what to do I'd be, like, mate, I could block your nostrils with a cotton bud so just stop. Not that I'm like that, I'm not aggressive, not massively anyway. Ty used to say I was passive aggressive in the classic British way and I was, like, no way mate, if I'm feeling aggressive there's fuck-all that's passive about it, I will shout about it, stamp about it and generally have a right old paddy until everybody knows exactly what's going on. He said I was wrong and the fact that I thought all that showed my utter lack of self-awareness. Bit harsh, I thought. But when you get to the fourth year of a relationship, that sort of shit gets flung around and you can't even be bothered to argue your side cos who's got the bloody time?

Anyway, on the window ledge that day, we had time. Cos we were twenty-five. We were unemployed. We were fed up with life and we were trying to find some adventure to grab without needing to have a bank balance filled up by days spent staring into nothingness on a swivel chair, surrounded by people you wouldn't save if the ground gave way and you had, like, stretchy inspector gadget arms or something. He was smoking. I've never smoked but I always wanted to. I thought it suited me, that deep breathing don't give a shit hid by big clouds of smoke type of thing, but my asthma disagreed and so I never did. We spoke for a bit about the warehouse. Where we'd backflipped, what we'd ran, he admitted he tripped up on the banister by the back stairs which made me laugh and I thought I'd never admit that, he must be alright. He was new. I'd been doing it for about four years. Since Dad moved away. My mum died when I was five and so Dad had always treated me like some sort of jelly bean in a party bag – dressed bright and colourful but wrapped in plastic, people advised not to take it out because the sugar content could drive you to do something crazy or convinced you (and by you here, I mean me), as the smallest jelly bean, to stay wrapped up and let others get picked first cos the likelihood is you get picked out and before you know it some clammy hand drops you on the ground and you get squished. Finished. No more you.

Yeh he's a bit crazy. I get my analogies from living that sort of life for way too long. When I was twenty-one, Dad announces its time he moves on. Decides I'm old enough all of a sudden to be let loose and off he goes to Mexico to live with some mate he knew from school who has a surf shack and turns out Dad at sixty saw himself as a surfing type, he'd just never realised it, as he was from Bolton, which is about as un-surfy as you can get. Anyway I was, like, get in. That's sick. I stayed in our flat, could pay the rent with a four-day-a-week bar job while I figured out what to do with my life. I did *not* want to get to sixty and realise I was supposed to be a dog whisperer or something. I started parkour, free running, soon after that cos the bar I worked at made me want to kill people and parkour made me see how I could be strong without resorting to violence as a means for self-expression and empowerment. Yeh. So. There we were. On the window-sill and I dared him, Ty, to follow me through the window, speed vault over the water tank, dangle off the roof, jump to the ground – which he did. He bruised his knee pretty bad and after that he always wore pads. We were crazy in love. Pushing the boundaries of our bodies from building to building . . . and in bed. I'd never felt that sexually attracted to anyone before, it was insane. We didn't stick to the bed actually, we did it everywhere and anywhere we could get away with it. Makes me feel a bit sick now but at the time it was a whirlwind of wonder. Genuinely thought I would never ever want another . . .

There's an extra power you get when you know what your body can really do. Ty got better than me at that eventually, better at parkour than I could ever be, sponsorship deals and championships, and the dynamic changed a bit between us, I wasn't so excited about sex or about him in general anymore. I still loved him, it was just different. He used to get upset about it but I was, like, this is what you wanted, you wanted to win, you did win, you can't have everything. And you can't. That's just how it is.

Susan   After I had Ty, I realised I couldn't have everything. It wasn't possible to maintain my aquatics career and give him the care he needed from me. People said that it was, but of course it wasn't. That's just how it is. As a woman. You do what you have to do and I had to take care of my Ty. I still wonder if it is really me in those photos. Me in a swimsuit. A body like that. Eyes as shiny as the fabric that stuck to my breasts and not my stomach. That's just how it is. Now, I bake. I do it well. I have a few bestsellers, my clients are mainly women I know from various clubs. I've taken some time off at the moment, obviously. But today. Today I baked some very special cookies because *she's* coming round. I want her to feel at home here, welcome. She is, she is *very* welcome here.

Mona *is on the doorstep now, looking at a cactus plant in the porch.*

Mona   He bought his mother that.

A giant, prickly cactus plant to put in the front porch. Tells you plenty about the sort of family they are, I always thought. Who puts a cactus, a giant one at that, in the porch? Not very welcoming, right?

I ripped my tights on one of those killer spikes once and Susan, her response was something like, 'I'm sure you've had worse things strike you in life, my dear', her eyes daring me to say one more word about the absurdity of having an armed and dangerous plant parked up close next to the front door.

Your legs are the problem, not that plant, that's what her syrupy smile said.

Bloody Susan, never a hair out of place, all high street twin sets and sugar stuck on to actual sticks for tea. His face used to light up like Brighton pier when he'd drag me along to see her, despite all the stuff he told me about her, he was all hugs and 'whens' and 'whys' and 'oh, I've been *dying* for one of your cookies, Mum' –

She stops in her tracks, realises what she has said. Can't carry on, brushes off the emotion.

I wore jeans this time anyway,
I usually do, the last time was a fluke.
I'm armoured, against the plant,
it seems to have worked.

2

Susan   Sit down, Mona dear, we don't want your veins to become like ravines, do we?

Mona   Ravines? No. Nope. That would be –

Susan   Tea? Would you like some? It's here, ready and waiting.

Mona   Sure. Thanks.

Susan   This is just regular breakfast tea, although loose leaf. I have others if you'd like.

Mona   That's fine, thanks.

Susan   How have you been then? I thought I would see you before now, it's been a week since we –

Mona   I . . . wanted to give you some space.

Susan   Space. Yes. That's what Ty always said. Preoccupied with finding more space.

Mona: Yeh, well.

Susan   I forget, Mona, do you take sugar?

Mona   Please. Just the one. Milky too.

Susan   Right. Very good. Here we are. Cookie?

Mona   Are those – ?

Susan   His favourites? No. No I don't think I could – not yet, anyway. Maybe one day for . . . (**Susan** *looks towards* **Mona***'s stomach.*)

Mona   Right, well, I'll take two then, cheers.

Susan   Oh please do, you have to make sure you're getting enough sustenance, Mona.

Mona   I am, thanks, Susan. Eating like a pig, which is pretty normal for me really.

Susan   Well, good, I suppose. Personally I haven't had any appetite since the . . . accident. I've perhaps eaten three bowls of corn flakes and a few flapjacks in two weeks.

Mona   The flapjacks your sister made for the wake?

Susan   Er, yes.

Mona   Yeh, man, they were tasty. Although I'm not sure about that amount of raisins – raisins have always seemed to me to be a little bit weird don't you think? Like wrinkled bits of the kind of black snot you get if you go on the London tube – (**Susan** *looks at* **Mona** *and she realises she's going off on one*) – anyway, yeh, you should eat, Susan.

Susan   Are you still at the . . . flat?

Mona   Um. no, I've been staying at my dad's. He's not there for a few weeks, back in Mexico for a holiday, and our flat, mine and Ty's, it's – is a bit intense, you know, all our stuff thrown all over the place, like he's gonna walk back in and I'm gonna nag him about picking up his socks and – (*she is upset*) – sorry, um, yeh so I can't face . . . clearing it out . . . just yet.

Susan   I was meaning to. Don't take this the – I would like to do it, if you don't mind.

Mona   Clear the flat?

Susan   Yes. Of Ty's things anyway. You can – do what you want with yours, obviously. I . . . it would mean a lot to me.

Mona   Course, that's cool. Just don't say I didn't warn you, some of his stuff *stinks*!

Sorry. I keep trying to make jokes cos I think it'll help but it doesn't really. Sorry. I'm sorry.

Susan   Would you like more tea?

Mona   I'm good, thanks. So . . . how's Adrian doing?

Susan   Back to work now. They needed him and he probably needed it, to be honest. I'm just moping around here and it's not yet garden weather, so it was getting him down, really. To be expected, such a shock, it was.

Mona   Yeh.

Susan   You know, I never thought there could be a worse pain than giving birth to Ty. I was in labour for four days!

Mona   Ow.

Susan   Quite. Two days at home and two days at the hospital. Back then, they wouldn't even let you walk around. I was strapped to the bed, my legs up in stirrups, everyone and anyone who walked into the room could just sit and look right, you know . . . between my legs. I mean it was awful. Adrian wasn't even allowed time off work so he was only there in the evenings. I refused all the drugs. They thought I was mad. When Ty finally arrived, I'd experienced so much pain I couldn't even see him clearly, I just heard him crying, and I thought, thank God, he's going to be okay and then I blacked out. It's . . . one of the reasons we never had another. Not wanting to go through that again. (*Starting to get teary.*) But it was nothing. Absolutely nothing compared to the day he . . . the day he was . . . when I put that phone down, the whole of my ear was on fire. Then the side of my face, my teeth were like knives stuck upwards into my gums, my torso writhed with tornadoes, my toes scalded my own feet. It was hell. Right here, in this living room. I lived through hell.

Mona   He . . . loved you more than anything.

Susan   Mother and son, there's nothing that can break that bond. You'll find out, Mona, when our little angel is born, I know it's a boy.

Mona   Um. About that, Susan –

Susan   I know. You'll think me presumptuous. But I just know it, Mona. I have a feeling in my bones. I've had dreams about it, about greeting this new little boy to the world and feeling like Ty is with us again, oh, it's just too wonderful a prospect I get so carried away, I've already picked out all of Ty's old blankets and toys that I couldn't bear to get rid of from the attic and anything you need, anything at all, you know me and Adrian will take care of it? You know that, don't you, Mona?

Mona   I do. But, Susan, um. Well. This is really . . .

Susan   Have I offended you by predicting a boy? Did you both want a girl? Is it too much to talk about right now? Oh, I'm sorry me and my big mouth, it's just –

Mona   No, no, it's . . . it's fine. But I really have to tell you . . . Oh God this is . . .

She does deep breathing.

Susan   Mona, what is – you're scaring me –

Mona   I'm just going to have to say it really quickly okay without breathing and –

Susan   Oh no, oh God, please don't tell me there's something wrong? Have you had a scan? You're too early for a scan aren't you? Did you bleed? It doesn't always mean the worst, you know, it can be all sorts of things, it can be stress – and you have had a lot of stress, in fact we all have, haven't we? We've all had so much stress. Recently, I mean.

Mona   Yes. About the stress. No. About the other stuff. Listen, Susan – please listen and don't interrupt, just for a few seconds, sorry I don't mean to be rude, it's just I'm . . . Okay, alright, well, what I came to tell you is that I'm not actually having the baby.

Susan   Excuse me?

Mona   I'm not having the baby. In fact, I'm, er, I'm not even pregnant anymore.

Susan   Any . . . anymore?

Mona   That's right, not anymore.

Susan   Mona. I'm sorry. Not pregnant?

Mona   No, not, not pregnant. That's right, Susan.

Susan   I'm finding it a little hard to . . . to . . . to . . .
(*Gasping.*)

Mona: Breathe?

Susan   Understand . . . what, what . . . it is you're saying.
Please, say it again.

Mona   Um. Look, I know it's not easy. But the thing is, it
was just timing, and after –

Susan   JUST TELL ME!

Mona   Woah. Okay. Maybe I should come back. I can go
over the, um, details with you when things are less . . . raw
and maybe we can have –

Susan   Tell me why the fuck there is no baby.

Mona   Like, I came here to share this with you, so just . . .
take it easy, yeh.

Susan   Tell me, Mona.

Mona   I . . . I had a . . . We . . . we had a . . . termination.
Two days before . . . before Ty's accident.

Susan *struggles to contain her cries. Her head is in her hands.
She's rocking.*

Mona   Susan?

Susan   But he . . . he told me. He rang me to tell me and he
said he was . . . happy. You were happy.

Mona   He lied, Susan. I'm sorry. I told him I didn't want to
keep it and he called you in front of me, sort of like a – a
threat, I suppose, or, I dunno, I guess he wanted to try and
show he had some power in the situation – but it was well out
of order and –

Susan   You're going to give me all the details.

Mona   I am, I mean, that's it, what I've said –

Susan   I need to know everything.

Mona   Well, that's it really, what I've said, that's all there is, I mean I didn't tell you sooner cos you know, I knew you were happy about the baby and devastated about, you know, and it's all been so –

Susan   *All* the details. About the . . . the termination, abortion, the taking away of the baby.

Mona   Foetus.

Susan   Grandson.

Mona   Cells.

Susan   I want to know e*verything*.

Mona   I . . . I'd rather not, to be honest, Susan. I get it, you being upset, I knew you would be, but I don't wanna sit here and tell you – I mean, that's it, I've told you –

Susan   You've told me there's nothing left. Maybe that's why he was so careless, why he fell, maybe it was because of that, oh my, have you considered that, Mona, have you?

Mona   Susan, that's not fair.

Susan   Fair?! Are we going to discuss what is fair in life now, Mona?

Mona   Do you want to punish me?

Susan   I just want to know.

Mona   But if I'm saying I'd rather not go through it all and you're making me feel like I have to, it's sort of like you think I deserve to be punished a bit. Do you think that?

Susan goes to a corner of the room. **Mona** *delivers the following to the audience.*

Mona   Right. Yeh, I should be punished for making a responsible decision. It's a fucking joke. We can't win. Cussed for being irresponsible enough to have kids without stability and then cussed for being responsible enough to take the action needed to not have those kids. Shit.

What is it with people who think they have some rights over my body?

My flesh isn't like the dough you use for your double choc chip coconut cookies, Susan. You can't just grab it, flatten it and push it through a metal mould, you know? I'm a human being not a bloody Great British Bake Off ingredient.

*To audience – picking up one of **Susan**'s cookies?*

Mona   The thing about cookies, right, is that they crumble. Everyone knows that, always have.

So why the fuck would you dedicate your life to baking them?

There's some cookies you get, when they're properly fresh, they've got a chewiness, a melt in the mouth moment to them. I like that, every now and again, but come on, man, you're gonna *die* soon, live dangerously. Baking is, like, the epitome of safe living.

Trust me, if you'd stood on top of a thirty-storey building, ready to jump across a two-metre gap to the next roof, knowing if you slip that'll be the end of you – you'd realise there's no need for tea, for cookies – *life* is out there. In the mess we've built.

Concrete and glass set up for our bodies to take back, for us to stop being frightened of the things that are meant to fit *us*, not the other way round.

Nature – *that's* something to fear, that mother is *the* mother. There's no tricking or hiding from her.

But our nature, the one built up by greed and pride, we have to know how to navigate it otherwise we're only ever living a half-life, right?

She picks up a photo frame of Ty? Or just takes a moment to pause and reflect.

I miss Ty. I do. I miss his too-tight laces on his trainers. The way he'd speak so calmly and politely to everybody, even the most rudest person in the world would start being all nice.

It's only been two weeks. Feels like he could just be on a trip. He never went on a trip. We laughed a lot. Which is travelling of sorts I reckon.

We argued too though, that day we argued non-stop. I'd told him I didn't want to keep the baby, he was saying don't be so hasty, it could be a great thing blah blah, and I was, like, nah Ty, I know myself, okay? Maybe one day but not these days. And he's, like, don't I get a say? And I'm, like, not really no, cos it's my body and it's my life –

I'm the one who gets left holding everything if you decide to go.

He goes mad at that, like how could I think that of him? It's not some sort of Luther-like investigating hunch, is it? I tell him.

It's what I've seen, what I've lived, what I know. So. He holds that up as his trump card, my hard-heartedness, my unwillingness to believe a man can sacrifice to the same extent as a woman.

Then, well.

He tells his mum, right there in front of me, I hear her screechy little scream of joy, her breath stopping on the speakerphone as we all know she wants to ask *you are going to get married*?

But doesn't.

It must have taken all the strength in her tea-stained liver to stay quiet on that one.

I hate him with every cell in my body from then. Men go about life with no idea what it's like, to constantly be on edge that even the one you love might try to mug you off, make you his punch bag or, worse, to be constantly on edge that when you walk down the street you're not seen to be wearing anything that could put you in danger, it is your responsibility to not get yourself into danger and you know what I mean by danger, don't you?

To be constantly on edge about contraception, having to ask for it to be used, being made to feel unfaithful if you do, or using pills every day even if you're not having sex for years, hormones all over the place, bleeding when you're not supposed to, overflowing sanitary towels and ballooning tampons, and we like to think this is because we're sensible about not wanting to catch any infections but really it is because for our entire lives we are made to be constantly on the edge about getting pregnant.

About not getting pregnant too young, about not leaving it too late to get pregnant, about not being able to get pregnant at all, to make sure you eat and drink the right kinds of things for if you do decide to get pregnant you have the best possible insides, to accept that your career will take a hit if you become pregnant, to know that your career won't progress to the top if you don't, to only get pregnant to someone you love, to do anything in your power to become pregnant, to definitely don't get pregnant until you're ready, to never be ready to be pregnant, to be ready to lose all the weight when you're no longer pregnant – he didn't have a single thought about any of this, until aged twenty-nine years old a girl he lives with shows him a blue stick.

Says, I'm pregnant.

And he decides that if he can't decide what she does with her body he'll try to – to what? Bribe me? Shame me?

Make me keep it for his *mum*, who I don't even like? I told him not to come home that night.

To piss off and get a grip and read up on some women's rights.

He told me I was a spoilt bitch and left.

The next morning I booked an appointment for the morning after that and Ty came back and was all screw face about it but agreed to drive, they said someone had to drive –

Susan *turns back around now, talking to* **Mona**.

Susan   I could have trained the British Olympic swim team. For Barcelona 92. It would have been a dream. Ty was three years old. Never wanted me to go anywhere without him. But I thought I'd be able to sit him in the buggy at the side of the pool. He was good at watching, not too noisy. But it's echoey, isn't it, a place with a pool? People were kind at first. Some of the assistants took him for walks round the grounds. Until he bit a receptionist's finger so badly they couldn't type for a week, after that he was left next to me at all times. The swimmers, they weren't the final team at that point, they were competing against each other, it was tough. A child's cries ricocheting on damp tiles wasn't the most productive audio environment for elite athletic training. Adrian refused to take the time off and I tried childcare. It cost all of my wages and made Ty unmanageably aggressive. I quit. And in the end, the team only brought home one bronze, so I mean it wasn't exactly like conquering an empire. But to me, it would have been . . . nice. My aquatics career remained something to fit in around Ty. Teaching children, so I could put him in the pool too. Elderly classes, I could do whilst he was at school.

By the time he was five, he was in so many sports clubs and after-school classes, I thought I might as well give it up, concentrate on him being the happiest he could be. Adrian agreed. I'd trained in pools since I was twelve. I missed it. But Ty excelled.

That sort of life, you and your child, held together by every single thing you couldn't do and every single thing they wanted to do, it is . . . satisfying, but . . . Ty was my entire life, Mona. Now he's . . . gone and inside of you was the one thing that could let me know that my whole existence was not a total waste.

Mona *is awkward, not sure whether she should hug her or not. She feels quite emotional after that outpouring. She goes towards her, but never quite manages to touch her.*

Susan *looks at* **Mona**, *urging her to begin. Maybe she does this at any point when* **Mona** *hesitates throughout the following.*

Mona   We drove with the radio on. Radio 1. I like 1xtra but Ty always took the piss, said that was for kids. I can't remember the songs that were on. We were in the car for about fifteen minutes. I cried for all of them. The tears started out silent, you know, just brimming like they do when you think you can hide it, tell people you've got something in your eye and they'll believe you. But I couldn't stop thinking about myself. I wasn't thinking about *it*, about the baby, I was thinking about me. Who was I to decide I didn't want this baby in our lives, in my life? What sort of crap person was I to be twenty-nine and still not be ready, not be anywhere near ready for a baby? Was my life so great without it? I wasn't happy anyway, so why would a baby change that? If it did, maybe it would change it for the better, but then, like, I'd be having a baby to make me happy and that seemed like the saddest thing of all. The tears grew and the sounds came, you know when you just can't tame them, not that I hardly ever do that. Ty parked up, he turned his head to me and said, *if you don't stop crying the nurses won't let you go through with it*. He switched the engine off. No hug or hand touch or anything like that, just the facts. Sorted me out sharpish though, thought – and I'm sorry Susan – but I thought, yeh, stop crying cos imagine having to have a kid with this bloke, bloody Samaritan of the century. But then he – he did put his arm around my shoulder when we buzzed in at the door. Inside there were loads of people. Like a waiting room for housing or something to do with bureaucracy – waiting and waiting but not knowing what you're gonna get told. That was the atmosphere, which was weird as I guess, like, people did know what they'd get told. They knew why they were there, but it was, like, we didn't, too.

Most of the girls – the women – they were there with a man.
Few weren't. I wondered about them. Thought it was
probably nicer to come alone and not have to worry about
why someone who should be holding your hand wasn't
holding your hand. Some lady who looked like she'd rather
work at a Ladbrokes than there took me upstairs. Ty had to
wait. She laid me down on some sort of lounger thing. Like
the premier seats at the cinema that everyone nicks when it's
not busy, sort of semi-reclined-type thing. There were
women all around me on similar seats. Some had just come
out of the surgical procedure, I knew that cos they were all
woozy and I heard the nurses talking to them about
aftercare. Others were doing what I was doing. Holding a
white plastic cup by the ridges in the middle, gripping it
until the orange squash inside made the shape of a bow tie
and being handed two pretty big pills wrapped in plastic.

Susan Pills?

Mona Um. Yeh. It's – it's what they recommend, if you're
under eight weeks pregnant, instead of the surgical
procedure thing. It's supposed to be the better option but
well.

Anyway. So. The nurse sits with me whilst I have a sip of
squash. I mean I haven't even drunk squash since I was, like,
six, and I have to put this pill on my gums, underneath my
top lip. It bubbles and fizzes and she says wait until it melts
completely, then leave. She tells me to do the same with the
other pill once I'm in the car. She asks how far away we live.
She confirms that by the time I get home, it will start. It
sounds harmless, but the taste of the pill is bitter. Bad.
Chunks of acid seeping into my bloodstream, making my
teeth freeze, too late to say no, to take it out, you have to
continue now, there's no stopping, the white powder is
working its way to the baby in the making to make sure it's
not ever a baby and that's what I wanted, that's what me and
Ty went halves on the 500 quid for, that's what I told the
nurse hundreds of times until she could be sure it was ethical

to sign and it was, cos I was sure, I am sure, but that doesn't mean that the taste of a decision even if it's the decision you know is right tastes nice, does it? Let's just say that it wasn't good, sitting there with a propped-up lip, a big old pill fizzing around the inside of my mouth, a nurse with stern eyes and puddles of smile lines staring at me, checking I didn't spit it out cos then the job wouldn't be done and who knew the damage that could be done, it had to be done properly. Finally it was gone. The first pill. I felt the same. Bit sick, but the same. She gave me a biscuit. I didn't eat it.

Back in the car, Ty started the engine and I put the second pill on the other side of my gums this time. The side of my lip that he couldn't see. He was being sweet. I can't remember what he said but he touched my hand when he went to change gears and he wiped underneath my eye when some sneaky tear escaped so I thought maybe it wouldn't be so bad after all.

By the time we got back to the flat I was doubled over like a compass. I got into the bathroom and didn't leave for the next five hours. Ty brought me water and food that I didn't ask for, but I could see he just wanted to help, he felt helpless as I screamed and cried, it was like nothing I'd ever felt before. The bleeding – are you sure you want to know all this?

Susan   Yes.

Mona   The . . . bleeding wouldn't stop. Clumps. Blood clots and clumps and I was seeing stumps of limbs even though I knew they wouldn't be formed yet, I saw them, my eyes swimming with so much red, red everywhere, wriggling around on the floor with a belly exploding with all the unfairness of the world, I hurled myself against the walls, determined to stand up, man up, get a grip, Mona, you're the sickest freerunner about but it was too hard. And you know, you know that phrase 'man up', it's a load of crap. I know that now having felt that scorching of my insides.

By about midnight the pains were subsiding and the
bleeding got less. It didn't stop though, not for a week, even
though they said six hours tops. Sleeping was hard. Every
few minutes a new thump to the stomach, which was better
than every second. I supposed that was it, by then. The baby
was in the sewage system. Flushed away with all that red. I
mean it *was* all that red, that's all it was, it was just blood and
cells and stuff so yeh. It was just red.

*There's a moment of silence in the room. Sadness. The next speech
happens almost as if* **Susan** *is hypnotised at first.*

Susan   It was as if the entire pool had gone red.

The bright blue we were all used to had just been swapped
as if it were nothing more than a filter on a theatre light,
replaced with a brazen red, an infiltration of unwelcome
colour nobody had expected. The children started to
scream. They thought, quite impossibly, that a shark had
entered the pool and bitten off a few legs or arms or
whatever it must have fancied in order for these clouds of
red to be billowing around their own legs. They checked,
they still had theirs and they used them to kick to the sides as
quickly as they could, helping each other up and out, which
I found quite touching.

It took me a few seconds to figure out what was happening, I
must admit. When I did, I think a small scream of my own
joined the children's, though thankfully nobody would have
been able to tell. I looked down and, sure enough, there was
my very own hell swallowing up my torso, flowing furiously
from below my waist. Thick, viscous red. I told the children
to wait by the showers. There was no shark, I said, don't be
ridiculous, it's just a cut on my arm I had from gardening,
the plaster came off. They didn't argue, relieved, thankful,
laughing now.

I came out from the pool, half mermaid, half devil. I had a
white towel. I always used white towels. I did what I could
with it, wore it as a cape to escape the inquisitive kids trying

to catch a glimpse of my 'gardening injury'. The blood still flowing from between my legs, covering my feet as if they were webbed in red rubber and I am always thankful to the young lifeguard, a teenage boy, who saw what was happening and called for some help, other staff taking the children to their lockers and parents, a note of apology sent out the next day. I went to hospital. A miscarriage. I was eight and a half weeks pregnant. Ty was five.

I didn't want to try again. Adrian was . . . pushy, but I refused. It was too . . . bright. That blood. They had to drain the entire pool, close it to the public. The real story got around, of course. Most of the parents – mothers, obviously – they were quietly kind, understanding with friendly smiles and little shoulder shrugs when they saw me. Others left, unashamedly. They didn't give a reason but perhaps they somehow saw what had happened as marking me out as irresponsible. Somebody who couldn't keep her own baby inside of her should certainly not be allowed to keep the life of mine in her hands, especially not when it comes to water. Water can be so very dangerous.

Another silence. **Mona** *looks around uncomfortably but clearly moved by the story. This time she manages to reach* **Susan** *and she puts her hand on her. They manoeuvre into an awkward hug at first, but then this becomes quite genuine and emotional.*

3

Mona *is now standing outside the house again.* **Susan** *is in the living room. We can see them both.*

Mona *is bent down, as if tying her trainer laces.*

Mona   Ty always said I wore my laces too loose. I suppose there is some sort of comfort, feeling the leather press close to your foot like this. I feel like I could run for days and days and days.

Susan *is holding a blue swimming hat.*

Susan   I get my hair done every week. It's one of those luxuries I never cared for before but, as life changes, so do the things you hold dear.

She handles the swimming cap longingly. **Mona** *is tightening her laces. As she begins to stand up,* **Susan** *begins to put the cap on, stuffing her groomed hair into the cap, not caring and smiling as she does it.*

We are left with the image of **Susan** *in her swimming cap in the living room and* **Mona** *standing with tightened shoelaces.*

With a Little Bit of Luck

This dream of a project began at the Bush Theatre with Madani Younis and Omar Elerian, attempting to create a UK Garage musical set over a summer adventure with three friendships at the centre. Michaela Coel took part in the first R&D and brought some crucial, illuminating feedback to the story which made me aware that the way the script had developed was not the story I really wanted to tell. I wanted to centre on one girl at a transitional point in her life, at the time when UK Garage was at its peak, in London. Due to various scheduling reasons, the project moved over to Paines Plough, where I was able to team up with the director Stef O'Driscoll, who I'd wanted to work with for years, and she was able to read what I wrote and let me know exactly what I needed to edit to get it to where she thought I was trying to get it to, plus had an equal love of raving and music and an incredible ear for intertwining it with a story. Such a joy. I gave birth just before this went into rehearsal, so I wasn't around much in the room, but raving along to it at the Roundhouse with 1,000 other people was definitely a career highlight.

With a Little Bit of Luck was first performed on 16 July 2015 in the Theatre Tent at Latitude Festival with the following cast and creative team:

Nadia   Seroca Davis

Vocals   Martyna Baker
Musician   Gabriel Benn
Direction   Stef O'Driscoll
Lighting   Prema Mehta
Sound   Dominic Kennedy
Costume   Grace Nicholas
Movement   Yassmin Foster
Producer   Francesca Moody
Assistant Director   Nadia Amico
Production Manager   Jayson Gray
Stage Manager   Hamish Ellis
Assistant Lighting   Martin McLachlan

1

There are three performers on stage.

One is a young woman, she is the **Actor** *and plays multiple roles.*

One is a DJ (called **DJ** *in the text for ease), who plays a mixture of acoustic and electronic music throughout – mainly adaptations of original UK garage tracks (all of which are listed throughout).*

One is a a singer (called **Singer** *in the text for ease), who plays in support of the above and sings with the vocals from the original songs, which can also be interspersed creatively with words from this text, to emphasise particular moments. This is at the discretion of the creative team, as is the decision to have a soundscape in places where no song is indicated.*

* (*Bracketed italics indicate stage/musical directions*)

* *Normal italics indicate direct speech within the narrative*

* Normal font indicates narrated narrative

(*Pre-show the* **Singer** *can be singing a mix of garage songs if the audience are sitting in there.*

As the lights come up, **DJ** *and* **Singer** *go straight into a lively, recognisable but altered version of:*

Summer of Love by Lonyo

As this plays, **Actor** *is dancing around what is presumably her bedroom and getting ready – patterned clothing, big jewellery, slicked-back hair, sunglasses etc. Holding each item up, posing, sometimes singing along. Choose the lyrics from the song that seem the most interesting and relevant. The audience should want to get up and dance already.*

Once **Actor** *puts on her sunglasses, the music cuts out abruptly and she turns to the audience.*)

2

Actor   That song there, it's why I'm (*turns around to* **DJ** *and* **Singer**) why we're here.
Not just that song alone, although it's a good one.
Lonyo, Summer of Love.

I saw some shoulders going, I know which ones of you are already in this. But for everyone else.
We are here because of garage.
UK garage music.
The music that made us dance with hope in our hearts.
And summer. The summer of 2001.
And love. The timeless kind, for all kinds of things.

So when we begin, because we haven't really begun yet,
this is the whole get you comfortable
let you know what's going on bit,
I will become a different version of myself.
Maybe me in 2001. A mouthy little wannabe undergraduate called Nadia with a love of syncopated beats
and heart-expanding, logo-laden drugs.
I will on occasion also be a few people who aren't really anything like me,
but they're important to what happens to the me
(who's not really me but Nadia)
at that time and to the time itself,
so I need to show you them and I need you to just go with that.

There's a musician (*introduces* **DJ** *by name*).
You could dance to what she/he does. Or the shoulder skank still holds strong, even the gun finger salute (*demonstrates both of these*).

Then we have the mellifluous (*introduces* **Singer** *by name*).

Together, we are going to take you to June 2001.
(*This could be a good place to start the* **Summer of Love** *track again, or parts of it.*)

The summer before the twin towers went down in flames
and we still thought America was mostly good.

To London streets with their too slim pavements
next to roads tiled with traffic.

Windows down, tunes blaring out, smoking Benson &
Hedges before going home to watch the brand-new channel
– E4.

To the year Labour gained a landslide victory with a leader
who smiled a lot, used to be in a band
and would become a world expert in conducting illegal wars
(though nobody knew that yet).

To a university campus off a central street
in the heaving capital city.
To a paint-peeling office with plastic chairs
and a desk piled high with papers

To a girl standing in tight jeans,
waistband digging into her sides,
hair stuck down in a shiny parting.

A girl who is being told she has an unconditional offer
to study Business Management in September.

This girl – Nadia, nineteen years old – is over the moon,
this is the start of her BOOM boom boom new life
of living like she's gonna do something special, cos she is.
The admissions officer squints and says,
Alongside the government's commitment to pay the tuition fees
of those from low-income single-parent families,
which you, er, fulfil,
you can also apply for a student loan towards living expenses.

Excited to the tips of her false nails with the news of her offer,
she hops on a trial bendy bus to Tee's house –
he's her boyfriend of a whole eight months, basically life –
she knows he will get funny about her going to uni,
but of course he's got no reason to be
so Nadia isn't gonna take any grief.
Is she?

3

(**DJ** and **Singer** *begin to play the very recognisable melody of:*

Gotta Get Through This by Daniel Beddingfield

Actor *is standing with her arms crossed, obviously having some sort of stand-off/argument.*)

Singer   I just got to get through this.
I'm gonna make gonna make gonna make it through.
If I just get through this.

Actor   *Shit, shit, shit.*

Singer   Give me just a second and I'll be alright.
I'm gonna get through this,
I'm gonna get through this,
I'm gonna make, gonna make, gonna make it –

Actor   *Tee. This is a wicked opportunity for me, university, the first in my family, to study Business Management as well, I'll definitely help you sell all those bags and that you've got, I'll make a proper business plan.*

Tee can't express himself like Nadia can,
he just knows that he is supposed to feel like a man
and he feels right now like Nadia can do everything
he can never do no matter how much he tries.
If the world wasn't so hell bent on gender roles he would cry
instead he sighs and tries to make light out of it –

But Nads, you don't even like reading do you?
You got to do a lot of that at uni I heard,
so like, maybe allow it, just work with me,
we'll make paper me and you,
be a power couple like Jay Z and Beyoncé –

Beyoncé's going out with Jay-Z?!

Yeh, apparently.

Whatever, listen, Tee – course I like to read, I love to read, how can you not know that?

Nadia says this in a way she hopes is convincing.
The thing is, she does love books, but she loves beats more.

(**DJ** *and* **Singer** *begin to play their version of:*

Love Bug by Ramsey and Fen)

Actor   It's magic.
It's where everything starts,
heartbeats in the womb
that BOOM BOOM BOOM BOOM,
making us feel connected to something else
for the rest of our lives. Connected. Yes.

Books are good. Nadia likes metaphor and subtext,
argument, instruction, theories
and all the rest of it.
But a dancefloor?
There's nothing abstract about a dancefloor.
It's a physical place you have to get to, be on, look
forward to.
Moving to music, it's like a memory that's deeper
than any revision can dredge up, it's like summer on your
skin, it's like freedom you didn't have to fight for, it's like –

love.

Which takes us back to my little love bug, Tee.
Yeh, I know, bare cheesy, but why not?
I'd been single for the longest time when I met him,
my heart skipped a beat, I whispered to my mate –
Mate, he is so. Damn. Buff.

Tee is not really called Tee. Obviously.
But he hasn't told anyone his real name in about ten years.
Even his mum calls him Tee.
Tee always has a pattern shaved in to the side of his head.
Nadia traces it with her fingers when they're in bed.
She has one arm round his waist, one arm up,
fingers following the lines
his barber mate makes new every week.

He calls them art. She don't disagree.
Loves the smell of his soft skin as he wriggles closer to her
when she gets to a spot that tickles, then he jumps up,
brings her tea in bed.
Tea from Tee, just how I like it,
two sugars and so milky it looks more like cream.

Both of them nineteen years old,
deep under a duvet made up of dreams.
Dreams that are real, they can feel them.
They don't seem nervous about life
cos they know they're gonna make it. Or at least Nadia does.
Of course we will make it babes, like how can we not?
Whatever they want to do, it's there for the taking.
Tee wants to be an MC.
A bit of a cliché, maybe, it's like every boy
Nadia has ever known wants to be an MC or a footballer.
The difference with Tee is, *he's proper good*.
His notepaper flies out of every spot in his room,
lyrics written for the night he'll finally get on the stage
take the mic and everyone will crowd around bigging him
up.
In that world, with smoky fluorescent stages
and sweaty dancefloors
Nadia thinks that
anything is possible
and she loves that feeling,
that
anything is possible,
possibly any thing is,
is anything possible,
possible is possible
is
anything
possible?

Do this and we're over.
I love you like hot food Nads, yeh
but I need you by my side,

not off studying with some posh guys
and all that.

Her rational brain knows that what he's saying is a load of
crap.
She wants to shake him into being a normal human being,
but he's had a bad few years, she knows that more than
anyone,
and they do have so much fun together.
Nadia puts her hand on Tee's arm,
the gold ring he got her for her nineteenth bursting with
hope.

Ok look, I don't want you to be mad at me, or sad, or angry.
But just hear what you're saying.
I wanna do this for us, for me and my lovebug.

His muscles soften. She smiles. They kiss.
He pulls away to say,

I can't change my mind on this babes,
can't explain why, just think on it yeh?
You should know as well,
if you and me ain't a thing,
then there's no way I can bring you in
on all the fake bags and that we're supposed to sell.

Bloody hell. That's bribery right there.
She'd planned her year's money based on working with Tee
to supply the local markets with fake Gucci.
Yeh, she doesn't have a plan b for money this summer,
but she wants more than anything to be an entrepreneur,
anyone who doesn't want that for her too, well –

Singer   I gotta get through this –

I'm going out babes. Wait here for me yeh?

Nadia nods slow and then shakes her head instead,
feeling strong about what she's about to do.
As Tee gets to the door,
she speaks in a voice she likes the sound of:

This is my life. I love you Tee, but I won't have you dictate it.

Singer   I'm gonna make, gonna make, gonna make it –

Actor   *I'm gonna take it, Tee, the place. At uni. I'm lucky to get it. It's what I want.*

Tee slumps against the wall. Sparks his spliff.

Okay cool, if that's it, then that's it innit?

Tee inhales, can't see through his tears,
he won't look up out of his fear
at that face he adores
as he leaves.

4

(**DJ** *and* **Singer** *start a version of:*

Ain't No Stopping Us by DJ Luck and MC Neat

The lyrics of the song intersperse with the start of this section.)

Actor   It's true,
no-one does it better, trust me.
Sam, she's a hot-shot promoter, one of the best in the scene.
Ain't no stopping her,
no-one can do the things I do.
Always high-heeled black leather boots, whatever the weather.
Immaculate make-up, shiny eyes
that reflect back lies like baking foil.
Ain't no stopping her,
no-one does it better.
I got a simple motto,
made up from the days spent on cramped buses
with a mum bent pint-sized from the weight of Iceland bags –
you gotta work if you want a merc.
And oh I do.
I'll come alive when I'm driving fast,
beige leather seats from the SL-class sticking to my thighs.

At the moment, I got a second-hand Audi TT.
But I want that merc.
So I work, hard.
Keep putting on raves,
best UK garage line-ups every week.
In clubs, on boats, in bars, bowling alleys, so-called palaces –
wherever the people will come to and the music will play,
there's no stopping ME.
I started small –
always just the best DJs and MCs,
strict dress code on the door, you know, don't get it twisted.

(**DJ** *and* **Singer** *start some sort of tune, perhaps based on the bassy bit of:*

Scrappy by Wookie

for the following to go over:)

Singer   Gucci, Avirex, Patrick Cox, Armani.
Iceberg, Prada, YSL, Burberry.
D&G, Missoni, Moschino, Nike.

Gucci, Avirex, Patrick Cox, Armani.
Iceberg, Prada, YSL, Burberry.
D&G, Missoni, Moschino, Nike.

Actor   *Tonight, is one of my biggest events yet.*
Four years after I started, so close now
to the SL class – a convertible even,
all the tickets have been sold, the venue will be heaving.
Queues outside around the block.
Bring it on.
I show London how to rave OIOI haha.

This morning Sam meets Nadia at this new coffee shop,
I'm obsessed with it, it's called Starbucks.
Over caramel lattes they catch up.
They met a couple years ago when Sam was looking
for pretty girls to go on the front of the flyer for her new
night. Nadia was a bit young, but she fit just right,
so a guest list and a wrist band and

Sam had found herself a new brand ambassador
who eventually became a close mate too.
Nadia is completely in awe of Sam,
man, she is just **perfect,** *ya get me?*
She's got an Audi TT for fuck's sake,
imagine taking that around London,
windows down, seeing boys lean out their cars
and be like, yeh mate, whatever, haha!
Being able to stand at the front of rave queues
and say who can come through,
to have money to spend on the heaviest garms,
to carry power like that in your pocket, yeh man, I want it.

Sam knows she's a legend, she's worked hard to be,
not many girls in this scene who can say that,
so it's a position she intends to keep.

As Nadia explains about Tee, university,
about needing more money
than she can get from a student loan and a Saturday job,
Sam's phone rings and Nadia envies the little Nokia,
she's got an Eriksson that's like a tower block stuck to her.
Sam locks off whoever's calling,
her head is spinning with a plan
to get Nadia (and herself) balling –

Babe! How about – and don't get prang –
you start shotting little ones at my nights,
like, protected and that of course –
you keep all the profits cos I'm not in need of them.
I can see from your . . . bag and nails, you are, big time, ya get me?
So you get all pimped up and
I'll have a shotter I trust in there
giving people proper pills only, no dodgy laxatives or whatever,
meaning my nights get a rep for being the all-round clever choice
and you get enough paper to redecorate your life with.
Result or what?

Nadia thinks not.
Her tongue is stuck,

she can't talk back to this rapid-fire plan
that's jumped out of her idol's mouth,
plus the cusses about her bag and nails catch in her throat,
she studies Sam's face for signs that it's a joke. No.

Er. Yeh, sounds heavy but um.
Well.
I mean, I could get time.

Sam licks the last bit of frothy milk from her lips,
smiles at Nadia like she's a little kid –
in fact there's only four years between them –
and bends down to pick up her Gucci handbag.
Nadia knows it's a real one,
not like hers that has 'E's on it instead of 'G's.

Nads, you'll be protected yeah?
That's what bouncers do, they know the drill.
Anyone else gets caught selling pills, they get chucked out,
any police come sniffing about we'll throw them a false lead,
you'll be free to do what you want, spend what you want,
wear what you want, uni or not.
Sam hands her a number written on a parking ticket
and five twenty-pound notes.

Here, we'll start small.
Think of it as a loan towards your higher education.
Ring this number, he'll give you 100 for a quid each,
see how we go tonight.

Tonight?!
Nadia tries to speak but nods instead.
Sam smiles, tussles the top of her head and leaves.

As Nadia's about to follow Sam out, say
allow it babe, I'm not on it you know,
she sees the Audi TT through the window.
Shiny and sleek, Sam getting in all sexy and chic,
engine revs up and Nadia toughens up,
don't be so weak, girl,
you gotta take risks to get what you want in this world.

5

(**Singer** *and* **DJ** *begin their version of:*

Over Here by M Dubs Ft Richie Dan

This continues (as do all of the songs?) through the following scene.
Emphasis on 'Over here. . .over here. . .'?)

Actor   Nadia waits in the shadows of a corner.
Shaky
Flaky
Faking –
Give a shit
Breathe
This is me, blud –
Fate
Chance
Dreams
Pull up
Big up
Fix up –

Car pulls up,
tune vibrating loose gravel
beneath her new Nike TNs.
It's all over quick,
the mate of a mate of Sam's hands over
the wrapped-up-in-masking-tape bag of pills
that will give her some sort of dream world.
Her hands leave one hundred pounds
plus clammy prints on the black leather seats,
she hopes the guy won't notice the last bit, he's quite fit.
And that's it,
the package is packed deep inside her bag,
she walks tall, feeling the whole world just within her reach –
watch me show the whole world how big I can be
I will be skyscraper high
limousine long
smooth as a first-class flight –
but for now, let's start the night.

6

(**DJ** *and* **Singer** *begin their version of:*

Closer Than Close by Rosie Gaines)

Actor   Nadia is close,
closer than close,
to a few girls she's known since she was a kid.
She doesn't hang about with people from college,
just these girls, her closer than close girls,
they'd grown up in London,
knew the way it breathed grey all over you
if you didn't keep moving,
they always moved.
Now they sit in the sun on a picnic table outside a pub
where slot machines and one-pound offers frame all angles.
Nadia is quiet about her and Sam's new plans for the
summer.
She sips vodka lime and soda,
laughs at her mate's story of waking up with a boy
she didn't know,
but wonders secretly if maybe she's outgrown
these closer than close girls.
She's done some calculations,
with the right situation
she could be making thousands
by the week – the week!
She can see herself in a VIP room
sipping Laurent Perrier Rôsé,
wearing top to toe Dolce & Gabbana.
Looking around her, these lot just didn't cut it.
Her Erikson beeped.
It's Sam, checking the pick-up had all gone to plan.
Nadia shakes herself out of being a right bitch,
goes to buy them all a round of drinks,
cos let's face it, if she goes to prison,
these are the lot that will visit.

7

(**DJ** *and* **Singer** *start their version of:*

Poison by DJ Luck and MC Neat ft. Shy Cookie)

Actor   *Poison.*
That's what Sam thinks boyfriends are.
All hers have been so far anyway.
I got one at the moment, big name DJ.
He's vexing me every week
expecting to get the best slots at my events,
I've told him nuff times I don't do favourites, babe,
I go with what's best for the night.
Recently that's started to make him act like –
poison.
Saying things that aren't nice
wouldn't sit right in a convertible Mercedes
with beige leather seats, do you know what I mean?
So in-between confirming
all the thirty-five bouncers needed for tonight,
the out-of-work model doing the VIP list at the door
the guy supplying the smoke machines for half price,
I think I just might finish with him,
when I have the time.

Couple thousand people will be in here soon,
all moving to the music they love.
It's a music I love, trust me,
have done since that time four years ago,
at a jungle rave
when I drift past a smaller room,
a room with smarter-dressed people inside and I heard this –

(**Singer** *and* **DJ** *start their version of:*

Never Gonna Let You Go by Tina Moore, Kelly G Vocal Mix)

And I'm in there,
cropped sweat top and trackie bottoms

out of place but I don't give a single shit,
sing along,
hands in the air.
I could never let it go, never get enough.
Not much has changed, to be honest.
Fun, money, power, love.
I'm not sure I will ever have enough.

8

(**Singer** *and* **DJ** *start their version of:*

Girls Like Us by B15 project

Focus on the 'Girls like this' lyrics. Can continue throughout this scene at different volumes/tempos etc. as appropriate.)

Nadia hides half the pills in her room.
She's a girl who's pretty good at hiding places,
had a lot of practice.
I just unpick the hem of the curtain
string the pills in long thin tubes
wrapped in clingfilm from the kitchen,
sew it back up.
Material's thick enough,
you'd have to touch it to spot anything's there.
Well clever, if I do say so myself.
One of her girls is coming over,
to get ready together,
share perfume, laugh together
compare Moschino, drink together.
She won't tell her about the pills hidden in the hems,
or rest of them she plans to stuff in her bra
and the front of her pants to sell tonight –
won't tell **nobody**.
Her mum is on a late shift,
she works at a local caff.
Nadia's never been proud of that.
When she comes home smelling of chips and beans

Nadia wants to scream at her *you deserve a better job, Mum*!
Always looking after everyone with what little she has,
Nads loves her mum to pieces,
but she knows she can't – she won't – let her own life be like
that.
The bell rings,
the girls get ready, sing,
sip brandy and lemonades, wait for the cab.
Nadia makes sure her pills are flat-packed
in the front of her pants.
A small tube of them also in-between the labia –
they're wrapped up well, there ain't no, let's say, extra flavour,
for any of my buyers. Haha.
As soon as she gets in there, she'll unwrap them
into her little plastic baggie,
put that in her fake Prada satchel
and the cash in her bra,
in the slots where the push-up pads would usually go.
Cab's here! Let's go!
Nadia feels the nerves,
butterflies of excitement, expectation, everything
flow all around her limbs
as she distributes a pill each to her and her girl,
they down them with the last of the drinks,
before laughing themselves in clouds of perfume,
out the door and into the looming London night,
Nadia feels like she's been waiting for this her whole life.

9

Tee is already there, waiting.
He's smoked his way through one spliff and two fags,
jittery as he goes over lyrics in his mouth.
I might get a chance to take the mic
in one of the smaller rooms tonight
I wanna be ready, need the chance,
need Nadia to see me up there,

see I'm worth a fight,
worth more than some dumb uni course.
I want to be up there,
getting his voice heard, his lyrics reworked
by the happy jaws of fellow ravers.
He's early cos he's hoping to catch
Nadia's mate Sam rushing about outside,
hoping she won't yet know they've broke up,
if she does, hoping she'll listen to his plan to get her back,
let him in round the back, no entrance fee.
He sees her, calls over,
Sam has no time for him,
puts her hand in his face and says
twenty quid or piss off,
he pays up as Nadia and her mate pull up,
all glittery skin and gold earrings.
Sam waves them through,
Nads is looking beautiful, thinks Tee.
She doesn't glance back at him,
even though she sort of wants to,
this is no time for distractions, she's got work to do.

10

(*Lights could change to show they are now deep in the rave.*

Singer *and* **DJ** *have begun their version of:*

With a Little Bit of Luck (We Can Make It Through the Night) by DJ Luck and MC Neat

This can be something that can be heard in various forms throughout the play?

Actor *is dancing. Let this play this out without talking until there's a big drop?*)

Actor   Two pills in now.
Two.
Down.

Up.
Definitely up.
Lucked out.
These pills are good, man.
Luck. Good luck.
She loves luck. Lady luck.
Heaven, she's in.
Am I?
No.
She's in London.
Lucky.
She loves London.
I fucking love London.
Smile.
London winks.
Eyes wide.

(*The track is mixed by the* **DJ** *and* **Singer** *into:*

Gabriel by Roy Davis Jr

At the point of these lyrics, **Singer** *and* **Actor** *come in together,
although* **Singer** *is singing and* **Actor** *is speaking the words – can
also interact/dance etc.?*)

Singer & **Actor**   Dance-ing
soon became a way
to
communicate municate municate municate
feel
the
music deep in your soul
Ga-briel playing, playing
hold on, hold on –

Actor   This isn't just young people releasing
frustrations, energy and pain,
this is bodies balancing their heartbeats as one,
transcending into places they've been told
they weren't born to tread in,

reconnecting to the air around them
by putting their skin into as many molecules as it can fill
and
oh babe, I fucking love you
smiles wide,
lipglossed kiss on cheek,
mimes – ('*There's something in your eyes*' *– sung by* **Singer**)

(**Singer** *and* **DJ** *start their version of:*

Something in Your Eyes by Ed Case (K Warren mix)

Lots of the below has lyrics from the song, so **Singer** *can interweave with* **Actor** *as and when appropriate.*)

Actor   It's at these times here Nadia has no fear whatsoever,
she knows it's all a race, but she may still win it,
look at this, all these people, from the same crap places as me,
but they all have
something in their eyes
a look you can't deny
ambition, hope, expectation
she can see the signs
theirs will be the time
when finally people who have always been far behind
will win the race
cos
there's something in their eyes
a look that never lies.
Look, she says to her mates,
dance with me
feel the beat
move shoulders
feet one step to the side each
back again
hips swing
hands move
conducting like it's you who made this track
because you did
now dig down

pout, smile, no frown
eyebrows up
fingers straight
top of ribs to bottom of bum
move it
nothing stiff
just lift
let it go
heart knows the rhythm
born with it
won't look stupid
flow
knees bend
go down low slow
arms to your head –
yehhh!!
(*Everything comes to a big climax musically and physically.*)

11

(**DJ** *and* **Singer** *begin their version of:*

It's the Way by Future Underground Nation

Perhaps start off instrumentally for a while and then the 'it's the way, it's the way' lyrics come in at certain points throughout the speech of the scene below – **Singer** *singing alongside* **Actor** *speaking?*)

Actor   Sam is having trouble with a few things.
Lively people dancing on top of speakers;
flimsy ceilings heavy with smoke falling on heads;
a diva DJ boyfriend to dump
and a high-as-a-kite Nadia to help do her first drug deals,
I mean, sheez, life ain't easy but
it's the way, it's the way, it's the way.

It's the way, it's the way, it's the way
Tee is about to see all the ways
in which his life could be a dream.

A DJ he knows in the third room needs an MC,
asks him, Tee, little him,
his face is all shock surprise happiness
now he needs to find Nads, makes sure she sees.

It's the way, it's the way, it's the way
the warm feeling round her neck
eyelids heavy
chest expanding
heart pounding from fingers to toes
back teeth grinding
can't stop smiling
Nads is not doing what she's supposed to.
But who cares?
This is it.
This is where the dreams are,
right here, right now,
this.

Sam shows up, pissed.
Nads, what you doing?
Shotting, not skanking remember?
Come on, get a move on.
You gotta work if you wanna merc.

12

(**DJ** *and* **Singer** *start their version of*

Hype Funk by Reach & Spin)

Actor   Movements of her mouth feel fuelled by cotton wool,
Nads moves around the dancefloor,
trips on dropped bottles,
repeating repeating
pills pills pills
until she makes some sales
walks taller, less buzzing now, looks around,
feels the crowd, hot spots for sales

where
there
yes him
her
gurning turning
take those
score please mate
wait, have an extra on me
enjoy have a good one
scuse me please
oi watch it yeh
Tee grabs her arm
don't you dare –
You cool?
Wants to think *'fool fool fool'*
but those are the lips she kissed for eight months
the creases at the sides of the eyes she saw cry at *Toy Story 2*
so she lets him get close to her ear
whisper that he misses her
I'll be on the small stage in ten minutes
holds her hand, feels a load of bagged-up pills
what is this?
Nadia smiles, proud of him, glad for him
missing him, smelling him,
bringing her lips to his neck
she can't resist,
can't keep her hubris in check –
my university fund,
no shitty shop job for me.
I bought a hundred Tee.
look, do you want some?
Tee takes the two she hands him,
can't stand how she's trumped him,
something deep down explodes at the injustice
You take the piss you do
all that talk of doing the right thing dreaming the dream
you're just a fucking drug dealer now Nads
is that what it's come to?

Just so you can get some poxy certificate to prove
you're cleverer than the rest of us?
Stuffs the pills in his pocket without a final remark
too scared his voice might crack.
All Nadia can think at first is
why the hell did I tell him about the pills?
Then she gets angry at his easy words
wary of the way they hurt
meaning truth was in there somewhere,
but what a dick,
he wants to ruin her life so she can be as miserable as him,
that's not happening –
she can throw some hurt around too.
Pills back in her bra, she finds the small stage,
she knows what to say.
Grabs the mic from the DJ booth,
hears her voice echo around the room as she shouts,

MC Tee, who you're about to hear, is bare shit trust me,
so if he stays on too long, ask for a refund yeh?!
She runs off, hears people laughing and jeering,
can't see Tee fuming and turning around on the spot,
he's not going on now, how can he, what for –

who the fuck does she think she is,
fuck it mate, this is war.

13

(**Singer** *and* **DJ** *start their version of:*

Destiny by Dem 2)

Sam is under attack from a to-do list
longer than her hair extensions.
She's on the way to the door
to see why one of the DJs isn't being let in,
when the one thing that can ruin her destiny
parks up en masse,
you have got to be having a laugh –

Nadia's on the way to the toilet laughing
about what she said about Tee
but feels a bit bad
cos he's not really a crap MC –
then a girl runs past, hooped earrings hitting her face
shouting
the feds, the police, they're all over the place!

If she can just make it to the toilets,
she'll figure out what to do.
The officers she can see look confused.
No gunshots are going off,
even though Trident said
plenty of the party-goers will be armed and dangerous,
so the police are weighted down with vests,
ridiculous next to the easy movement
of the scantily clad people
they're supposed to be saving society from.
So now –
Batons out,
would they use them,
yes.
Move,
let us past.
Pig.
Dirty pig.
Smoke, everywhere.
Hair in faces.
Turn around.
Ow.
Down. Legs.
Up, just empty cans.
Teeth kissed.
Kissed.
Kiss.
Don't miss the opportunity to arrest, arrest.
Lights up.
Fuck the po-leeese!

Rave is done,
officer in charge says so.
Go home.
No-one's hurt.
Adrenalin.
Breathe.
Smoke.
But we paid for this.
Shit.
Nobody gives a shit.
Out, now.
What the fuck,
watch –
Push.
Pull.
Up.
Down.
Sideways.
Sticky floor.
Don't fall.
All the noise.
Noise.
Lights.
No.
Lights are on?
Better get gone.
Run.
Stumble.
Right into the arms of an officer.
Stay right there, miss.
Nadia wants to cry.
Why? I need to pee.
Officer grabs her glittery arm,
come with me please.
Nadia's bra and pants pulsate with fear,
this could be the end of her.
No more uni, no more dreams,
no more anything,

except prison bars and bad food.
Put your arms up.
Up.
Gulp.
Help.
Just then a crowd come past.
Stay and dance, fuck the feds.
The officer gets pushed, she's pissed.
Forgets about Nadia, goes after the others.
Madness.
No music left.
Close.
Closer than close.
Closer than you ever could imagine.
Oh.
Nadia loses no time,
hurries to the fluorescent light
she can see seeping out from the grimy toilet doorframe,
she's been saved.

Stop.
Stop right there.
It's Sam shouting commands at the police,
not the other way round.
She got no warning of this raid
she doesn't pay anyone on the inside
she can't believe they would do this
I can't believe you would do this
to a woman's independent business.
Nadia doesn't think she can come out.
She found a utility cupboard in the toilets,
moved a few paper rolls and got herself into it,
closed the door tight and now she's stuck tight.
No music, just the sound of her tinnitus,
occasional crackle of walkie-talkies
as police send bouncers and bar staff home.
She hides the twenty pills she has left under a mop in a bucket
won't part from the cash, nobody can prove how she got it.

14

(**Singer** *and* **DJ** *start their version of:*

Destiny by Dem 2)

Actor   Tee found some new mates back in the rave,
the MCs he's idolised since he was a kid.
They knew what Nadia did,
thought she was bang out of order for what she said,
let him spit some bars to them instead.
They liked what they heard,
so when the police came they pulled Tee out with them,
held a car door open for him as he ran
and he sat in the back thinking –
destiny, man, this is it, this is mine.
No thought for Nadia now, his buzz giving him only love
for these heroes he's surrounded by,
passing zoots and jokes around,
all smiles,
all high.
A couple of hours in, light streaming through the blinds,
the guy Tee had given one of his pills to asks,
mate, can you get us some more of them tings?
Course he can, he'll just make a few calls.
All that matters is things can stay like this,
Tee hesitates,
then dials Nadia's number off by heart,
no answer, no answer, no answer.

As the sun comes up and the brown river shines pink,
Nadia finally gets the courage to pull herself along sink by
sink,
out of the now-empty building and into the streets.
The summer air is warm on her still-glittery skin,
she walks home and can't stop thinking.

What can she do?
She still had fifty pills in the hem of her curtains.
She'd go with Sam to an out-of-town rave,
sell them for fifteen quid each to those twice her age.

Plus 100 quid still in her bra from tonight,
this plan would give her 850 pounds to turn her fortunes
around.
Reinvest in more supplies,
take it seriously this time,
avoid London, it's too bait,
make schedules of all the countryside raves,
places with more demand and less supply.
Yes, in between England's great green hills
there's masses of people who just want good pills.

15

(**DJ** *and* **Singer** *start their version of:*

Little Man by SIA)

Actor   Nadia puts the key in the door.
Looking forward to sugary tea.
Sofa.
Sigh.
Quiet,
don't wanna wake Mum,
she'll be up soon anyway.
Toes hurt.
Breathe deep,
maybe stomach some toast.
Butter only.
Yeh.
Pyjamas first.
Bedroom.
TV.
Table.
Bookshelf.

Curtains.
Hems.
Cut.
What the –

How
What
No
No
No.
Gone.
Every one of the pills – gone.
Not there.
Missing.
Taking up no space.
Just threads of ripped curtain hems
strung out all over the place.
Head shakes.
No no no.
My plan, my fucking plans, man.
On the floor.
Too drained to cry.
Why?
Or more to the point –
WHO?
Nobody but nobody knew about this hiding place.
Only two people know where the spare door key is.
Tee . . .
Sam!
Gets her phone out, sees a missed call from Tee, hours ago
now.
Text from Sam, *everything okay babe?*
so she sinks on to her single bed without taking her clothes
off.
Rage is in her fingertips, bubbling at the nails,
maybe it's true,
it's too hard to step out of the box you're born within,
her eyelids are heavy now so she sleeps,
boulders of betrayal battering her blinks.

16

(**DJ** *and* **Singer** *begin their version of:*

Battle by Wookie Ft. Lain Grey

There's lots of lyrics in this, not all are needed but intersperse the relevant ones as appropriate amongst the below.)

Actor   *So I'm flat broke.*
I refuse to answer the phone to Sam
and Tee's changed his number,
little shit,
I can't bring myself to knock at his door,
I just can't do it.
The shop I used to work at won't have me back
and everywhere I ask at takes one look at my gloomy face
and says 'we're not hiring at the moment, but thanks'.
Yeh, cheers.

With two months to go until uni starts,
Nadia has given up on the dream that things can only get better,
she hasn't even been raving,
can't face being there with no money.

Her mum offers her a job.
A daytime spot at the caff she's worked at for fifteen years now.
I don't understand how a 'yeh alright then'
comes out my mouth, but it does.
And I'm stood there all day pouring tea for old ladies
and buttering rolls for old men.
Stinking of chips and beans, so rank.
One day, as Nadia serves up milky milky tea,
she sees Sam approaching, breathes deep, *1, 2, 3.*

Alright there Nads? What happen to you?

Umm. I'm here init.

I been calling you. A lot.

Yeh, sorry, I got no credit.

No credit? So I guess you ain't got my ton either?

I will do, soon. Just . . . might take a while.

What about the dough from the things?

Shhh.

What man, these lot are all deaf. Tell me. What happen Nads?

It all went bad, Sam. Don't think I'm cut out for all these paper making plans.

You shoulda just answered the phone. I coulda helped.

I heard things were going tough for you too though.

Yeh, even more reason to pick up, stick together, thought we were mates? I don't give a shit about that hundred quid Nads, it was all for you anyway.

I'm . . . sorry.

They hug and Nads feels like she's light as dust.
Sam gets a tea and they take a seat.
I had to sell my car you know,
the five-o got all militant about the raves,
pretty much banned garage music in the city,
so I'm gonna start up elsewhere…
look, I was gonna ask if you wanna come with me?

Nadia didn't understand how a whole musical genre
could be banned from a city,
what exactly did they think it would do to national security?
But she did understand
that she didn't want to go anywhere with anybody,
not even her idol Sam.
Thanks babe, but I'm good here,
gonna do evening and weekend shifts when uni starts,
you know it's not that bad,
sometimes I even get tipped.

Nads opens her hand to show Sam a fifty-pence piece
and they laugh quietly,
well, it's a start sweetheart, I understand. Stay in touch yeh?

17

(**DJ** *and* **Singer** *start their version of:*

Sincere by MJ Cole)

One week before uni starts,
Nadia has been given more responsibility,
a bit of extra money for things like opening up or closing,
she likes that she's liked.
One morning,
she goes to open the caff up
and standing there to the side is Tee,
his face more stubbly,
his eyes shining with the wisdom of now being twenty.
His shoulders are slumped and he looks gentle,
she looks at him, stands still, but doesn't speak.
I'm sorry Nads, for what I did,
you know what that is.
I was mad, proper mad at you, you went deep on me.
No excuse still.
Anyway, listen yeh, with what I took from you,
I got enough cash and respect to get a recording slot in a studio,
it's all popping off Nads, I'm getting signed,
touring around the country and –
Nadia just stares at him, wonders how she loved this man.
Tee feels stupid, the way she always made him feel really.
Look yeh, I don't expect you to forgive me.
But I know uni starts for you soon, so I wanted to give you this.
Please.

He hands her a thin brown envelope. She hesitates then
takes it.

I'll look at it later, gotta open up now.

Um. Alright then, yeh, cool. You good though?

Yeh. Thanks for stopping by. Good luck with it all.

You too, Nadia.

He waits for more, she's got no more to give.
So he smiles the way that used to make her melt
and she nods like a boss,
unlocks the shutters.

Inside she rips open the envelope without turning the lights
on.
It's a cheque, no note.
She can just about make out the amount.
One thousand pounds. *One thousand pounds!*
What he stole plus a little extra.
I should probably rip it up.
Probably.
But 1,000 quid is like a whole month's worth of shifts,
serving 5,000 teas.
Nadia folds the cheque,
puts in it her pocket, it's time to open up.
Later that day, when her mum comes in for her shift,
she sits down with Nadia, gives her a bit of paper folded up.
Nads is a bit scared,
Mum what is it? Your face looks all weird.
Just open it luv, go on, open it up.
Nadia does.
Inside the paper is the second cheque of the day.
This one is five times more than the first.
I've been saving for years, for you,
I want you to have it towards life at uni,
I'm so proud my darling girl, I hope you know that.
Nadia's heart is about to burst,
she kisses her mum's face,
you know one day, when I graduate and make it big,
I'll be able to pay for us both to have the best life?
Thanks Mum, you mean the world to me.

Later on, she takes the other cheque and melts it in a pot of
tea.

Stares at the browning paper,
ink spreading into liquid,
What the hell did I do for that?
Shakes her head at herself,
but smiles too,
teapot in the dishwasher,
she's got things to do.

18

(**DJ** *and* **Singer** *start their version of* – **Celebrate Life by
Brasstooth**

*Starts off quiet during the narrative and gets louder until this song
ends the show in an uplifting moment of musical wonder!*)

For now though, in this autumn of 2001,
Nadia feels stronger than she's ever done,
knowing it won't be as easy as she thought it would be.
Stuff will always fuck up. And you got to be prepared for that.
Can't trust anyone except your mum, really, sad but true.
And no matter what, you have to look out for you.

She walks to the library of her uni
through the sunny city streets for a day of studying hard,
her bank card with a new student overdraft limit on it
in her back pocket.
She plans to spend it on some new garms,
it's too hard not to,
she might have realised some things
but she's not become a monk.
Sam's got her on the guest list
for all the best garage raves in the country,
she's got to look criss.
Nadia puts her headphones in
and feels ready to be who she wants to be,

these beats keeping her company,

(*MUSIC louder or grows in integration with text.*)

Feeling the power of being a part of something
that was made by people like her
and that's enough to get her through, for now.

End

Layla's Room

Written to tour UK schools with Theatre Centre, *Layla's Room* came from independent research I'd undertaken whilst facilitating writing workshops at schools and organisations across the country. I interviewed 1,000 self-identifying girls and young women about aspects of their lives and one of the main issues that came up, no matter what region they lived in or what background they came from, was sexual harassment at school. The government had recently held an inquiry into the issue and came up with a paltry response without any mandatory requirements for schools to take up to combat sexual harassment. I originally wanted to make the show 'magazine-style' in that each scene would be individual to itself and presented in a different medium, perhaps with a few crossover characters or locations. However, as so often happens with writing, timeframes, schedules, budgets and production practicalities made the more traditional route a necessity. The director Natalie Wilson and the actors did an excellent job of making the performances lively and varied, from school halls to community centres, and a recent amateur production in New York decided to have an entire youth group play Layla one by one, which I think would have been great to see. It's fascinating how many different ways the same piece of text can be interpreted and performed, so again, please take these stage directions to be the ones relevant to the original production and not essential to the story in every telling of it.

Layla's Room was first performed at Redbridge Drama Centre on 15 August 2016, with the following cast and creative team:

Layla	Shanice Sewell
Monica et al.	Emma White
Reece et al.	Alex Stedman
Director	Natalie Wilson
Designer	Ele Slade
Lighting Designer	Chloe Kenward
Sound Designer	Elena Peña
Dramaturg	Sarah Dickenson
Voice Coach	Joel Trill
Movement Director	Anna Morrissey
Scenic Artist	Andrea Siegertsz
Company Stage Manager	Vicki Heathcock
Production Manager	Pete Herbert
Set Builders	SetFree Projects

Characters

Layla, *fifteen-year-old girl, any ethnicity*
Monica, *Layla's best friend, fifteen-year-old girl, any ethnicity*
Reece, *Layla's potential boyfriend, fifteen years old, any ethnicity*
Joe, *new boy at Layla's school, fifteen years old, any ethnicity*
Mum, *Layla's mum, any ethnicity*
Dad, *Layla's dad (voice only)*

The above roles can be shared between three actors, with the actor playing Layla not playing any other character if possible.

One

Layla *is standing in her bedroom, which is in the process of being packed up for a house move. There is another girl and a boy on stage with her at all times, who will come in to play the other characters as and when needed. The action on stage is often* **Layla***'s memories being played out, but when she is narrating it is present time. The two states interweave constantly.*

Layla There's so much I want to tell you, but I'll start slowly. I've been told that sometimes I speak so quickly it's like people just see the words flick out from my mouth but they can't catch the sounds and then we go round and round with me repeating myself and them nodding and saying yeah, yeah, but then I ask what they think and they're like umm. So yeah. Slowly, Layla. My name is Layla. I'm fifteen years old and I'm about to move from the place I've lived in since I was born. I was born in June, the moon was full and my mum and dad were too late to get to the hospital so Mum had me in the kitchen, under a dining table we don't have any more, she said she found it comforting underneath the wood, but Dad said she was just trying to get away from him. He was joking, because at the time of my birth, they were best of friends, as close as me and Monica – were. That person you tell every crazy thought to, the sort of stuff you would deny till you died if it was in public. That person who makes you laugh till your sides slice. Monica always made me laugh so much . . .

Layla *and* **Monica** *are standing in the school toilets by the sinks.*

Monica Yeah so just hold on to the sink, like this, and squat . . . easy.

They squat, looking serious in the mirror.

Layla Um, Mon? Are we gonna do this for the whole of lunch?

Monica As long as we can I reckon.

Layla It makes my thighs burn.

Monica   Sort of the point.

Layla   School is stressful enough without making it some sort of army workout bootcamp that –

Monica   But think of the booooty –

She does a little dance with **Layla**. *They both laugh and start squatting again.* **Monica** *starts humming the tune to the below.*

Monica   I think two of my most favourite things must be singing and squatting.

Layla   I know, Monica.

Monica   Let's do the song? Come on. Pleeease?

Layla   Okay. Sixty seconds only. Let's go, B, you got this!

Music starts and **Monica** *goes into her own version of 'Independent Women' by Destiny's Child, joined in sporadically by* **Layla**.

Squatting: Tell me what you think about me
I bring my own lunch so I can make my bum lean
Do I only do it cos I'm feelin' lonely?
When lunch is over we get up and leave
Squatting: Tell me how you feel about this
Teacher says 'Don't do it' but it's worth the risk
Build my own bum so I can pay my own bills
Only ten more seconds left of this

The shoes on my feet
Mum bought them
The clothes I'm wearing
Instagrammed them –

Layla   Alright, B, time's up!

They laugh and stop.

Layla *is back in the room, silent and still.*

Layla   Monica is my girl, was my girl, I'm not sure where we are with our friendship right now, that's part of the reason I need to tell you all this, to figure it out, to know what to do. Cos what do you do when you're moving from everything you've ever known into the unknown? Into a ground-floor flat with a garden rather than the tenth floor of a brutalist concrete block which is locked with every memory you've ever stored, every hour you've spent bored or exhilarated, dreaming or singing or scheming or wishing you lived someplace else where there was a walk-in wardrobe and a cinema and all those things nobody really needs, but it's nice to dream, isn't it? Anyway, basically, this place, this flat, this block just by the best park in the world and ten little minutes away from school won't be my home after this weekend. Monday morning will be the first proper day of the summer holidays and the last day of looking out these windows to spy on the smokers and tokers and homeless and cyclists and happy kids down there, underneath my window on the world. Monday afternoon will be me looking out to a garden with grass and a small patio with those rippled grey slabs and I'll be like, thanks Mum, this is sick! But really inside I'll be crying, because it shouldn't have to be this way and she only did it for me, to get away. My little brother Kie, he's only three and even though he'll love picking up slugs from our very own grass, it makes me sad that he won't get to see, to really see, life from up here, like me.

Sorry, I'm doing the too quickly thing. But when I get to thinking, well, it's pretty stressful, isn't it, thinking. That's why I love having my headphones in, cos it's harder to think when I'm singing, even if it's just in my head. Beyoncé or Taylor or whoever it is that I might not admit I'm listening to, taking me away, making my mind stay a little bit still, moving to a rhythm instead of to worry and worry and – anyway. Today is Thursday and tomorrow is the last day of school and there's a big talent show like there is every July. Only Years Ten and Eleven can perform but the whole school watches. This is the first year I can do it. I've always imagined being up on that stage, staring into the hall, seeing a sea of people listening to my poems and just feeling so . . .

scared but amazing. I've been practising a few for months now, I wanna know them by heart, so it's like a proper performance you know, but . . . I probably won't do it, cos, well, it'd be weird cos like I'm not just leaving for the holidays but also, *for ever*. I mean, I'm not leaving school like a prodigy who goes to university early, even though I am pretty amazing at English and History, or like a well naughty kid who gets expelled and sent off and eventually crossed off from whatever list it is that keeps notes on those who don't do what they're supposed to. Nope. Not like that. Just like, as in, next term, I'll be going to a whole new school. It's a pretty extreme move. I've only got one year left, but . . . well, I wanna do well and to do that I have to move schools. To get on in life, I feel like I have to get the best grades I can and read every book that looks me in the eye and write and type *until my fingertips are flattened* – a bit dramatic, I know. I've always had a bit of a dramatic flair, maybe it has to do with being born under a kitchen table. It means I'm great for camp fires or boring parties or drama class but, well, when it comes to life / it's –

Mum   Layla darling, are you sure you're not exaggerating / this?

Layla   My own mother struggles to believe me sometimes, she thinks –

Mum   It's not so much that I think you're lying, Layla darling, not at all, more that – well, I know you like to add details / to make –

Layla   – details make a story. That's what I've learned from all the thousands, it is probably thousands, of books I've read in my life. But like, that doesn't mean just cos every detail might not be a hundrd per cent strictly true, that what happened didn't / happen –

Mum   I believe you, Layla darling, I do.

Layla   I do know, for example, that one time, me and Monica got caught shoplifting some lipstick. It's not

something I'd done before, but Monica loved doing these
selfie parties and we'd ran out of make-up to make us look
more likeable and of course we had no money / so we –

Monica   We went to the shops and there was no stopping
her, Layla, once she gets something in her head it's like,
that's it, she is on a mission. Determined, that girl is, I wish I
could be a bit more like that, but I'm so easily distracted / so –

Layla   Monica gets distracted by some cute boy buying
tampons – like hello, if a boy is buying tampons then it's
pretty likely he's got a girlfriend and that he's a decent sort
of guy who's unlikely to give out his number to any admirer
but whatever. She's just staring straight at him, not noticing
who's watching *her* as she puts some lipstick in her pocket
and the security guard swoops over and soon enough I'm
begging / for us –

Monica   I end up begging this huge security guard to let us
go home unpunished, cos my mum is ill – which was true at
the time – and if she found out she might die – which wasn't
so true I suppose but I had to save us cos Layla / was –

Layla   I was doing all the work because I felt really bad that
I hadn't shook Monica out of her daydreaming when I'd
seen what was happening, so I used all the reasoning I could
with the big guy in the small room full of CCTV. I told him
we were victims of marketing ploys to get us obsessed with
our looks and we couldn't be expected to afford the life we
were supposed to lead and / he –

Monica   He was sweet. He gave Layla a tissue to wipe her
tears and he said he didn't want to cause my mum any extra
stress, so he let us go with a twelve-month ban from all their
stores, but no police involvement, thank God, but that's
when / I knew –

Layla   I knew Monica's obsession with looks wasn't good
for me, so I started to lay off the selfie nights and trained
myself to not care about how many likes a picture got and
Monica was not happy about that. I guess that's when she
started seeing more of –

Joe   Joe. What's your name, beautiful?

Monica   Monica.

Joe   Do you like football?

Monica   Um. Yeah.

Joe   Who do you support?

Monica   Um. Whoever you do!

Joe   Ha. You're funny, I like you. Wanna come to my mate's to watch the match?

Monica   Yeah. Yeah, thanks.

Layla   Monica, we're supposed to be going out!

Monica   Oh come on, Lay, he's lovely, look at those eyes.

Layla   You don't even know him, he could be a –

Monica   Or maybe he's a –

Layla   You need / to be –

Monica   I need to go –

Layla   But what about –

Monica   Bowling can wait, babe, we'll do it another day. Don't worry, I'll Snapchat the whole way there, see ya later yeah? Did you hear him call me beautiful?

She walks away, waving.

Layla   You don't even like football.

I didn't kick up a fuss after that, even when it kept happening, cos I was glad for my friend, if she was happy, so was I, that's not a lie. We spent so much time chatting about having a boy in our lives who we actually really liked, so it was nice that she had Joe. It's just, he was, shall we say, a bit –

Monica   Pervy? Who even uses that word?

Layla   I say it, all the time, when we walk around town and grown adult men blokes lean out of their window and shout at us –

Monica   Yeah, okay, that's massively pervy, but Joe is like, the same age as us and –

Layla   He's new. Nobody knows anything about him.

Monica   For a new boy, he's doing pretty well, I'd say he's one of the coolest in our year now. Layla, you know, you don't need to be jealous, Reece will notice you eventually and –

Layla   This is not about jealousy, Monica, I just, it's the way Joe looks at other girls, even at the women teachers, it's . . .

Monica Layla's never had a boyfriend. She's fancied Reece for at least two years and she's still never even chatted to him properly, girl is *long*. I get it, she's threatened by my thing with Joe, but there's no reason to be, she's my B.

Layla   I can't really gather my words cos what she said about Reece hurts down there in the pit bit of the stomach. I get over it, but from that day, things are . . . If I'm honest, and I have to be honest otherwise what's the point of all this confessional-style stuff, it was the last afternoon . . . I felt like I knew who I was.

The next day – oh I forgot to mention this one little thing cos to me it really is just one little thing, like not even worth mentioning, just like a whatever, innit, but I have to mention it cos it became part of the story of why I'm standing in this nearly empty room about to move to a new place and wondering if I can get up on stage in front of the whole school tomorrow and say – sorry, too-quick thing again, right, so . . . The little thing is that my mum's gay, she's got a girlfriend called Aliyah and I really like her, she got me tickets for a gig Mum would never have let me go to for my birthday and she's just, like, a sweet lady innit. Yeh it was weird at first, I was like, '*Mum*, what the actual f – ', more cos

I was worried about what would happen to Dad rather than being freaked out by being thirteen and learning after all these years your mum was actually a lesbian. But Dad was cool about it, turned out he kinda knew apparently and after Kie was born, my mum couldn't lie any more and that was that. Anyway, this was ages ago. Stay focused, Layla. The reason I started on this is cos of what happened at school. The day after I called Joe a perv, Monica swears down she didn't tell him but then I heard at lunch this voice go:

Joe Oi, Layla, I hear your mum's a carpet muncher.

Monica Joe, don't –

Layla I think she prefers lino actually, Joe.

Joe Ha, yeah, you like a bit of banter, do ya?

Layla Is that your version of banter cos if so, I'm busy, mate.

Monica Layla, he didn't –

Joe I was wondering, yeah, like, just having a bit of a think last night before I went to sleep, ya get me, if that sort of thing runs in families and if so, like, when *you're* gonna have a go –

Monica Joe!

Joe What, babes? What I'm saying is, if your mate Layla here is looking to explore her sexuality and all that, needs a friendly pair of girly lips to kiss, then I was gonna suggest – you.

Monica Me?

Layla I'm gonna leave you two to your gif porno fantasies and go to –

Joe So what, you saying Monica ain't kissable?

Layla Mon, seriously, are we doing this?

Monica Answer him, Lay, don't you think I'm kissable?

Layla   No, I don't!

She runs off.

Monica   I thought it was jokes, we'd kissed when we were really little kids playing games anyway and we always cussed boys for trying to get girls to kiss each other in front of them so I thought Layla would get I was joking, she'd just be like, 'Oh shut it Monica,' and that would be it, but she went skitz . . .

Layla   I was so infuriated I went to the library and finished my English homework, some poem about identity, with more fire in my pen than I'd maybe ever had. I'd never been spoken to like that. So my poem was full of raging statements about why does being a girl mean shaving off leg hair and in adverts for razors there's no hair even there but they shave anyway and they're always that same shade of tanned like no other legs exist and that's before we even get to the armpits – there's deodorants that promise you beautiful underarms I mean, seriously, even the creases of our bodies need beauty treatments?

And there was a whole bit about why who you love or fancy is really nobody's business and why boys try to get girls to kiss each other, like as if even that can really only be for them and how grown men shout out of car windows when we walk home like we should know how to make our school uniforms less appealing and –

She stops, exhausted.

I stood up in English to read it. My teacher expected it, everyone did, I always read out my homework in English, I was good, everyone knew. From my seat, there he was. The new addition to my class. Joe, smiling at me with shiny teeth and narrowed eyes. I opened my mouth to aim my words all at him, though I doubted he'd be clever enough to get it, when he started pouting his lips doing kissing movements and the teacher could see, but she just shook her head, told me to read.

I sit down. I can't make a sound. I'm silenced and there's violence stirring in my stomach, my jaw clenched so tight I might break a tooth. Joe keeps smiling. The teacher asks why I've sat down. I don't make a sound. The class goes on.

Monica   Layla texts me to tell me Joe was making kissy faces at her in English class, all upset, calling him an arse and whatnot and I was a bit like, so what, it's a joke, he's new, he probably just wants you to like him, right?

Layla   In a bittersweet twist, Reece came up to me that day. Started our first proper chat. I'd semi-secretly fancied him since I heard his mum call him Ri-Ri at the school gates –

Reece   Layla, wait up.

Layla   Oh, hi, Reece.

Reece   I . . . er . . . I just wanted to check you're cool and that?

Layla   I'm fine, why wouldn't I be fine?

Reece   Um. In class. You're always, I mean, you're like, the star pupil and that. I like . . . listening to your stuff so . . .

Layla   Oh. Oh. Thanks. Yeah, I'm just, tired, I guess.

Reece   I guess she's not telling me the real story, but it's like, I don't know her too tough to start acting all like, tell me what's up Layla. I've secretly liked her since she did some sick poem about the suffragettes in history. She's different, she says the kind of stuff I think about out loud and that's, that's like proper inspiring.

Layla   I can tell Reece is kind. Not only that but he is like, my dream guy, cheesy as that sounds. But in the back of my mind as he talks I can just see Joe's lips moving round and I think, I don't want to get involved with a boy right now, what if he ends up like Joe?

Reece   So like, I was wondering if . . . maybe when you're less tired or whatever you could um, read me that poem?

Layla   What one?

Reece   The one you didn't in class, cos you usually do so –

Layla   I don't really like that one.

Reece   Okay. You got others?

Layla   Loads.

Reece   I could come round after football on Saturday?

Layla   I babysit my little brother on Saturday.

Reece   Sunday?

Layla   That's my . . . um, library day.

Reece   Okay, well, cool, like, maybe sometime.

Layla   Yeh, definitely. It was nice talking to you, see you tomorrow.

She makes angry-at-herself expressions when **Reece** *is gone.*

Layla Tomorrow is not a good day. Tomorrow is the day when the girl I thought was my best friend, who I've known since I was like, six or something, turns around to say:

Monica   Me and Joe think you should get with Ryan.

Layla   Rewind that, Monica, I think you're stuck on another planet's frequency –

Monica   Lay, why are you being / so –

Layla   When did you become such / a –

Monica   I'm just trying / to –

Layla   What is wrong with you!

Monica   What's wrong with *me*? Lay, I hate seeing you sulking around, your head down and your hair . . . a mess, I mean it was always a mess but like, really a mess and I feel like since I've been spending more time with Joe, you've . . . you've let yourself go a bit and I want us to spend more time together again so if you get with Ryan, then we can go out as a foursome which would be, like, amazing and we can –

Layla   She wasn't joking. She saw this as the solution to my apparent problems and her getting to keep her supposedly BFF and new boyfriend close to her chest, cos Ryan had become Joe's little sidekick over the last few months, but he was annoying and spiteful and I'd guess his brain was only half full so when Monica said I should get with him, after I got angry, I just sort of transported myself away from my body and looked at Monica from above, talking, talking, her nails done and her hair did and I didn't hate her, I just wished for the times when we could be doing anything and have fun, just us two.

Monica   I was just trying to find a way for us two to have fun together again. I'd only been with Joe a few weeks, but it was serious, we were deep in it. Ryan was alright, not like, earth-shatteringly fantastic, but like, alright – for the summer term at least, just so we could keep close, me and Layla, I didn't see what the big deal was, I'd have done that for her.

Layla   Monica passed on my refusal to Ryan and it didn't go down so well, in fact it seemed like him *and* Joe were attached to my back. They pinged my bra in the corridor, in the canteen, in the classroom, so immature.

Monica   Yeah sure, the bra-pinging thing is well immature, but it's like, boys innit, so course they do dumb stuff. It happens all the time. I'm surprised it hadn't happened to Layla before. I told her just ignore it, they do it to everyone.

Layla   I started to wear T-shirts under my shirt, even on the hot tropical-type days, to make it harder for their spindly fingers to find their way under my bra strap and ping it. They'd ring my phone all night, leave voicemails of one of them heavy breathing like weirdos, but they withheld the number so nobody could do anything and Mum said . . .

Mum   Don't answer if you don't know the number darling, ignore it.

Layla   Yeah, sure.

One day Joe and Ryan followed me home. Making moaning noises behind me, calling me –

Joe   Slag. Sket. Hoe.

Layla   I wouldn't run, kept walking slow. Then it got quiet and I was worried, turned my head a little to the side and bang! I felt arms grab me and pull me into some bushes at the side of the street, all scratchy and prickly and hands were running all over me and trying to get inside my shirt and . . . up my skirt and over my face and I was fighting them, I knew some boxing moves and I used them till I felt my knuckles hit bone and *then* there was a real moan and the hands fell away and I ran away until I got home and felt like I couldn't breathe.

So hard to breathe. Throat tight, lungs like a corset with the strings pulled in, desperate to draw air in. Stop.

Mum found me collapsed in a heap on the kitchen floor, near the very spot she'd had me.

Mum   My God, Layla, darling, what's wrong?

Layla   It's all gone wrong, Mum –

Mum   I'm sure it's not that bad, darling, come here –

Layla   'Come here. Come 'ere. Come.'

Mum   Don't pay them any attention.

Layla   'Do you want some? You want some. I know you do. I heard you do.'

Mum   You have to just ignore them.

Layla   'You love it like. You like it like.'

Mum   Don't even give them the time of day.

Layla   'Dirty. Dirty. Dirty little. Frigid little. Give me a little. Take a little.'

Mum   You're bigger than them. And you have to study.

Layla   Studying amongst boys who want to drag you to bushes is not the one, trust me. I didn't wanna make a bigger deal of it all than I needed to, I thought Monica could talk to Joe, sort it out that way.

Monica   Layla, the thing is, I think you might be taking this way out of –

Layla   You've seen it happening to / me –

Monica   You got a lively imagination innit, you need it, for your poems / and –

Layla   This isn't a story, Monica, this is real life, are you blind or / something –

Monica   Layla, all I've seen is some bra-pinging –

Layla   But I've *told* you the rest!

Monica   Joe's *told* me that before we got with each other you tried it with him / innit, so –

Layla   What?! That's a blatant lie, *me*, come on / Monica, you –

Monica   It explains a lot, yeah, you got to admit, so I'm not holding it against you, but I'm not gonna defend you against this thing you say is happening, but I don't see happening. If there's anything being said it's probably just a bit of fun, a bit of banter, you know how it is.

Layla   I know how it is.

It's sat in class too scared to put your hand up in case another hand grabs the side of your boob whilst you're trying to answer a question.

It's eating lunch in a toilet cubicle to avoid hands up your skirt on the lunch bench.

It's being so lonely you spend your breaks in the library cos everyone seems to think you're a lying liability and you'll get their boyfriends in trouble for harassment but guess what –

no boys get in trouble for harassment,
because nobody can see it happening,
it's just a bit of fun, a bit of banter,

Monica *and* **Reece**   You know how it is.

Layla I requested to my teacher to be moved from next to Monica in History. It was a big step, we'd sat together when we could for the whole of school, but I just couldn't pretend that we were all good. It shouldn't have been this that hurt more than all the other stuff I was putting up with, but it did. Monica pursed her lips when Miss said she had to sit at the back and she even kissed her teeth when Miss replaced her with Reece to sit next to me. I hadn't asked for that, it was a fluke, but I knew she wouldn't believe that, she wouldn't believe anything I said. But at least there was Reece.

Reece   So this History homework . . .

Layla   Yeah?

Reece   Shall we . . . work on it together, like, on Saturday or whenever?

Layla   I usually work alone.

Reece   Miss said we can work in pairs and . . . don't think bad of me yeah, but I, well I'm not too good at History so I'd love it if the star pupil could school me a little, do you know what I mean?

Layla   What do you mean?

Reece   What?

Layla   You say, do I know what you mean, like is that some sort of hidden . . . I dunno, like, I'm just asking what you mean.

Reece   I just mean, let's do our homework together, as a team, that's it.

Layla   He was smiling so sweetly and I couldn't keep being mean – I had to trust someone, didn't I?

Okay.

Reece came to mine and we sat writing and laughing and drinking milky tea and he said all sorts of lovely things about me being clever, like the cleverest person he'd ever met and I got all embarrassed so was like:

I'm really bad at maths. And music. Except listening to it. And I was accused of cheating in Physics cos, well, I did.

Reece   No way!

Layla   Yeah. I had to. I get them all mixed up, the gravity thing and the chemistry, periodic-table stuff.

Reece   Whatever, innit. I know that still, you're sick at all this school stuff.

Layla   Well – you're proper fit.

Reece   Oh –

Layla   Oh my God I'm so sorry that was like the most embarrassing, I was not meant to say that, out loud like that, I mean, even though you are, it's like –

Reece   So are you!

Layla   Oh . . . Okay. Right. Um.

Reece   Awkward?

Layla   Kinda. Yeah. Massively.

Reece   I'm . . . a bit shy usually. But with you, I feel . . . different. Cos you, you're . . . different.

Layla   Different. It made me tingly to hear him say that about me. And I wanted to push it, but I couldn't. Not with what was happening at school. Different. That's the word of the century isn't it?

Dare to be different, be yourself, be who you wanna be, don't be scared of being different – even if being different means buying and using the same product as twenty-five million other people. And they don't mean it. Cos when I started noticing other girls getting touched up at school and I said to them let's do something about it, let's report it, let's fight back, they were all like, nah, let's allow it, just keep the peace, it's not worth it, what's the point and I was like, okay, I'll be the different one, like Reece says I am. I'll speak out. So I did.

Mum   I'll support you all the way, darling, this has got to stop.

Reece   I'll back you up, Layla, that Joe boy is a bit of a knob.

Monica   You're gonna get a reputation as a troublemaker, Layla.

Joe   Ha you think some little report is gonna stop me? I'll catch *you* later.

Layla   Me and Mum at the deputy head's desk, the head was otherwise engaged. She's got a staged look on her face, pretending to be concerned but her head is half turned to her computer cos no doubt she's got too much admin to do to be wasting time with anxious youth, but my mum's good and she says:

Mum   With all due respect, I request that you take this much more seriously. My daughter's future is being put in jeopardy because you refuse to see that 'boys will be boys' is not an acceptable excuse to be using when it comes to anything really, let alone unwanted touching, sexual name-calling –

Layla   Hands up skirts, on backs –

Mum   In shirts, against walls –

Layla   Trip up and fall so they can see underwear –

Mum   Shall I go on? It's not on.

Layla   The deputy head nodded her head and signed a few forms to promise she'd look into it and she didn't look at me and Mum didn't look at me cos I could see there were tears in her eyes, she hugged me and said she'd tried. And I was naïve, I thought maybe they'd really do something.

Reece   The teachers said they were looking into Layla's claims, what had I seen? What could I say? I said Joe and Ryan have been a bit mean, I'd seen them ping her bra a few times, make kissy noises at her, smiling . . . funnily. I'd seen her crying twice but they were right, I couldn't say I'd actually seen with my own eyes much more than that, but I felt bad. I mean, I knew Layla wouldn't lie.

Monica   Layla lies. I told the teachers straight. I said she adds all this embellishment to her stories and they nodded cos they know this. Yeah, Joe asked her to kiss me and he pings her bra – big deal. He's been through a lot, he's got bare problems of his own to deal with at home, like why should she – and the school – make it more difficult for him? Adults always pick on boys like him.

Reece   Layla, listen, I need to chat to you quick.

Layla   What is it, Reece?

Reece   Um. It's not nice. I mean. It's hard for me to say this, but. I've heard some things and I know people chat breeze but . . .

Layla   Just say it, Reece –

Reece   Ryan's got a picture of you down on your . . . knees and he says that you were –

Layla He came up behind me and pushed me down! He must have had the phone in his other hand, I wasn't doing anything, please believe me, you of all people –

Reece   The thing is, Layla, even if I believe you, and I do, I do but even if you had I wouldn't, I mean it's not my – anyway, others might see me and you and think you're –

we're – you know, so it's probably like, better for you actually, if we don't hang out cos then, you know, they won't be able to say anything bad about that.

Layla   I couldn't even argue back.

Reece   I felt crap to be the one to tell her that, but it's better she knew. I didn't tell her they stuffed the phone under my nose kept saying, 'Has she sucked your little mushroom yet Ri-ri? I couldn't tell her that bit.

Layla   I felt sick cos that was it now. The photo was some rubbish fake that didn't even make sense if you thought about it. But the thing is, thinking doesn't come into situations like this. My grades started to slip. I didn't know the answers and what was the point cos I wouldn't get far anyway. How could I trust anything about myself when the two people I thought were the best turned out to be worse than the rest? What chance did I have out there in the world if I couldn't even manage to choose people in my life wisely, what good is it being good at school if you're doomed to be treated like a bit of dirt, what's the use of rhymes and opinions and imagination if you just spend your life being hurt?

To make everything even worse, Mum came into my bedroom to say:

Mum   The school say they looked into it and there's not enough evidence, no witnesses, they won't be pursuing it . . . So what do you want to do, Layla?

Layla   I want to wear a spacesuit to school, so I can float around and be untouchable and preferably it would have some sort of electric shock mechanism that would make any boys who tried anything fall flat on their back.

Mum   Well, we could ask NASA if they have any spare spacesuits but I doubt they'll say yes! So instead, I was thinking, I'd been considering it anyway and I'm worried about your grades, I'm worried about you – what about if we move?

Layla   It was the last thing I expected her to say. I said no way, obviously, stormed up to my room like a brat and sat in front of my mirror, staring at myself wondering if I could change the way life was going by being thinner or prettier or just . . . better somehow. I did my make-up the way Monica did, thinking maybe I'd blend in more like that, maybe I'd be able to get my confidence back. I stood there and said, Layla, tomorrow, you will get yourself back on track, don't watch that.

Reece   Layla comes into English with all this make-up on, looking all changed somehow. She won't speak to me any more anyway, so I don't say anything, but I know *they* won't let her new look go unnoticed.

Layla   My hand is up. I'm gonna stand up in class and read what I wrote for homework. It's a poem about loneliness as a response to what we've been doing on *Macbeth*. How madness can go unnoticed until it's too late and how hate can drive you to a really messed-up place. My hand is up. The teacher's back is turned. She has to go get something. Hands turn up around me.

There is a very choreographed physical moment here of groping in the classroom which is repetitive and builds and builds in speed and intensity until –

Layla *screams.*

Joe   It's just a game, Layla, chill out.

Layla   When he says that I wanna poke his eyes out. So before I can really stop myself, my fingers point and I push them into his eye – the teacher comes into the room, sees me doing that, Joe screaming –

Joe   Psycho bitch attack, Miss! She's trying to poke my eyes out!

Layla   Reece doesn't look up. I rip up the paper in front of me. The teacher tells me I'll be facing detention, I should be lucky it's not suspension, oh, and I shouldn't be wearing so

much make-up to school. Ryan and Joe laugh and she says
shhh to them, they don't.

Joe *is laughing.*

Layla   I can feel bile in my throat rising,
he size of my tear ducts growing,
a steel ball of pain in my belly bouncing,
flames of fury in my knuckles flowing –

I'm going. You can all piss off, I've had enough of this and of
you, watch out, cos one day someone is gonna do something
to you and there'll be nothing you can do –

Joe   Ooooh, I'm so scared!

Layla   I run from school and tell Mum, yes, yes, let's move.

Monica   Reece says he saw them do it this time, in English
class, and I'm like, but the school have already finished their
report or whatever it was, they're not looking into it, no
witnesses, Reece says he has witnessed it now, but I'm like –
the teacher isn't gonna lie and she saw Layla try to take out
Joe's eye! I dunno what's going on any more, I don't even
wanna call her, she's gone too far.

Layla   The teachers call. There'll be a report on my
attendance. Mum says the new school need me to have a
flawless report before I leave, I can't be skiving, my grades
can't be dropping, I can't be missing exams and coursework
but I ask her to just sign me off ill for two days, I need some
space, wait for things to calm down, she says okay.

Monica   I ask Joe if he did what Reece said he saw him do.
Joe starts telling me to calm down it was all just a game, just
a bit of jokes, bit of banter and if I don't get it then maybe
I'm just a dumb sket too and I'm like, I won't let you speak
to me like that, but then, I do.

Reece   I wanna go to the school about what I've seen but I
think they won't take me seriously cos someone will say I've

been getting with Layla or whatever, even though I wasn't and Joe and Ryan might get proper angry and . . .

Layla Dad calls me. He lives in Dubai at the moment, so I don't get to see him except on Skype, but he promises over the summer he's coming back for a while and we'll do all the things we love to do, like play basketball and go round Harrods's Food Hall looking at all the posh food we'd eat if we could and maybe now he's been doing this new job, he can buy me some of those cakes it takes someone a whole day to make cos the icing is so intricate and I'm like –

Dad, we're moving. I'm being harassed by boys in my class, like really badly and I'm not being ungrateful but I don't care about cakes right now I just want things to go back to how they were, I just want to stop being scared of going to school and I know you won't understand but –

Dad Layla, I do. I think it's a brave thing, this move. It will be good for you all. To move on. Change seems scary at first, but you and I know more than anyone, embrace it and it can be great. Plus, a garden! Beats my sandy balcony, ay?

Layla   I guess.

Dad   Listen, I want you to do something for me. Look in the mirror.

Layla *stands in front of a mirror.*

Dad   Tell me everything you see.

Layla   I see a stupid girl on the phone to her dad who's thousands of miles away.

Dad   What do you really see?

Layla   Me.

Dad   And who is you?

Layla   I wish I knew, Dad.

Dad   Try, for me.

Layla This is dumb.

Dad Act as if it's not you, it's a character in one of your stories. Who is she?

Layla She's . . . she's a fighter. A writer. A girl who beat her dad at football and basketball and all the sports they ever played. She's a loyal mate and a bit rubbish at the girly stuff like make-up and clothes and she doesn't see why those things have to be so important in life. She hates gossip magazines but she reads them at break time. She wants to change the world with words, wants to make people think about their actions and their lives and she wants to be more kind. She can be a bit selfish. But she's working on it. She's not the best sister, she'd rather sit in her room listening to music than play with her little brother. And she's sorry about that. She can be a bit of a brat. She hasn't asked her mum how she is for a few weeks, which is pretty crap. She'd like to be . . . stronger, famous, eventually, maybe – but not for something stupid, for something like changing laws or . . . or . . . I don't know. But she'll probably just fail all her exams and beg her dad to get her a job cleaning the sand off his balcony.

Dad Funny, the first half sounded a lot like a girl I know. You've just got to the end of term, Layla. You have to keep the good references and grades up and then you can stick your fingers up at all of them. Fight through till then, my girl, don't let them win.

Layla I love him, my dad. He does all this cheesy, self-help, motivational-speaking stuff, but you know what, it sorta works. I put the phone down and think yeah, who are they to make me pay for their miserable existence?

I get my stuff together, check my uniform's clean, take my seat in class the next day. The teacher looks pointedly my way but doesn't say a word. Nobody speaks to me the whole day. Joe and Ryan walk the other way when they see me. I hear sniggers and whispers but I don't care, if nobody's touching me or shouting names then I can do it all alone.

On the way home, I put my headphones in, smiling. I get to the part of the pavement just before the park. There's a boy in front of me. There's a boy to the side. There's another behind. There's Joe. There's Ryan. There's ones I don't know. Every spot I try to go to, there's someone there, blocking me.

A choreographed physical scene of **Layla** *trying to get somewhere and her path being blocked by the male actor (possibly both actors), with either purely physical movements or also with brief words that can be improvised. The action builds and builds until she is small and scrunched, though standing, in the middle of the stage. As they suddenly stop, she relaxes slightly as she starts speaking.*

Finally they stop. I'm standing in the middle of them all. Backpack on, headphones hanging out now. There's no sounds, not any that I can hear anyway. My ears are as blocked as

my path. I can't move. There's nowhere to go. I can only wait to see what they'll do. I can't fight this amount on my own.

I wish I could fly to the moon. They start to close in. I can smell them. Their suffocating aftershave. Their end-of-the-day breath. Their fear and their entitlement.

Ryan reaches forward first, pulls my skirt hard, down, another helps it along to the ground. I kick and shout but another starts on my shirt, to lift it, to rip it, it's all a mess everyone everywhere and me standing in the middle in my underwear, I'm in the street in my underwear, there, in my underwear, being leapt on by these –

Reece   Boys! What the hell you doing?

Layla   They scatter off laughing. I'm standing there, shaking, in my underwear. A car beeps. Reece hands me my skirt.

I put it on and I run. He shouts after me but I ignore him, I will ignore everyone from now on.

I will ignore the light
I will ignore the TV
I will ignore the magazines
I will ignore the phone
I will ignore the door
I will ignore ambition
I will ignore desire
I will ignore life.

Mum   Layla, darling, please open the door –

Dad   Layla, it's Dad, calling, again –

Monica   Lay, listen, I heard what happen and that was out of order, talk to me yeh?

Reece   Layla? Hpe UR OK. Luv Reece x.

Layla   I ignore and I ignore and I like it. Being alone in this room, the rain or sun or clouds against the window, my reflection ghostly, transparent. Exactly how I wanna be. I look at Twitter and Facebook and Snapchat and Insta and I just look. All the lives going on as normal, no videos posted of me in the street in my underwear. I feel grateful for that. Grateful. The fact that I feel grateful is too much for me, it makes me feel sick to my stomach. To think that's how low what I want for myself can go. When me and Monica were younger, well, like not that long ago actually, we used to shout our dreams for the future in the mirror – yeah, it might sound weird but my dad said it could make them really happen so we did it:

Monica   I will be a famous singer –

Layla   I will be a world famous writer –

Monica   I will fall in love –

Layla   I will be fluent in Spanish –

Monica   I will get the best-thigh gap –

Layla   I will make laws against the gender pay gap –

Monica   I will enjoy Shakespeare –

Layla   I will be cool when Reece is near –

Monica   My mum will get better –

Layla   Monica's mum will get better –

Monica   I'll never be without Layla –

Layla   At least Monica's mum did get better, that's the only one that worked. All that schoolgirl dreaming and the thing is I really believed I could do it. Now I'm just hoping to not be found semi-naked online and my mind can't stretch much further than that, making laws about pay gaps, practising my Spanish – sound like the wishes of someone else, someone I'd like to put my life inside but I can't find a way to even hold their hand. And I can't see much but the glare of screens or the screaming blank blackness when I close my eyes . . .

and I've never felt like this,
so desperate, so distant,
so depressed, so desolate,
so delicate,
it's like I'm not quite here,

even though I know I am cos I still need to wee and whatever, I even eat every day, but these things happen without my say so, my body going along with its business as though I'm not really a part of it

and I can't seem to snap out of it,

I don't know if my mum visits me, I guess she does cos I find her hairs on my duvet cover in the moments when my eyes work and I find plates of food on my desk and a letter from her saying how she loves me and I know she does I know she really, really does but it's just not enough. It's not enough.

I've had enough and I can't take any more. I open the bedroom door.

I'm going to get the medicine box and I'm going to stop everything, because what's the point of being someone you never meant to be, someone who is shrouded in so much dark she can't grasp her own dreams?

Better that I just sleep.
Just sleep.
Sleep. It will be like a long, sweet sleep.
Tears on my face.
Taking slow steps.
Knees wobbly.
Eyes bubbling.

Throat tight. No goodbyes. Kitchen floor. Cold. Cupboard open. Take the box down. Stretch. Tiptoes. Heel down. Squeak. There's a squeak. I jump.

The medicine box runs from my hand. I look down.

Kie's dinosaur toy. Yellow plastic with a green spine. Smiling up at me.

Kie. My little brother who adores me. He does. He really, really does.

I sit cross-legged on the cold kitchen floor and I hug that yellow plastic dinosaur and I sob and I sob.

Because it is enough. His love, my mum's, my dad's. It is enough. It has to be.

I start to eat with the family again. Spend time playing with Kie in front of the TV. Things are better, but I still won't go to school.

Mum   I have to send in all the paperwork for your new school place soon. You'll have to speak to them you know, darling, about why you weren't there for the final few weeks.

Layla   I hope they like fairy tales.

Mum   You could try and go in maybe, even for the last week? For the talent show and to say your goodbyes?

Layla   Mum, I can't even face that place.

Mum   You could say thanks to the head for allowing you to do your exams at home.

Layla   He should say thanks to me for not taking them to court for neglect of their safeguarding duties.

Mum   I agree with you, Layla, but I don't want things to be tough for you at the new school.

Layla   I think things will always be tough now, Mum.

Mum   Oh, my darling, how?

Layla   I dunno, it's . . . like, boys are . . . I see them and I think they're all the same.

Mum   Even Reece?

Layla   How do you know about Reece?

Mum   He's been knocking for you every day, Layla. You told me you didn't want to see anyone, so we have a little chat at the door and he goes.

Layla   Oh.

Mum   He's sweet.

Layla   He follows the rules.

Mum   Is that bad?

Layla   It is when the rules aren't made to be any help to us.

Mum   Then you should write your own, my darling. You have a way with words, use it.

Layla   Plus we're moving anyway so whatever.

Mum   You might be moving, but others aren't, darling, what about them?

Layla *is affected by this thought.*

Layla Later, the doorbell goes. I'm on my own. I decide to answer it.

Reece *is standing there, very awkward and shy. He mostly didn't expect her to answer.*

Reece Hi, Layla.

Layla Hi, Reece.

Reece I just wanted to say hi, see how you are, it's been a while so –

Layla Eight days.

Reece Yeh.

Layla Did you tell my mum?

Reece About what?

Layla About . . . what happened, you know.

Reece No. Doesn't she know?

Layla No, Reece, I don't want anyone to know I was stripped to my underwear in the middle of the street, thank you.

Reece I told Monica.

Layla Like she'd care.

Reece She does. She's sorry, we're both sorry, we . . .

Layla You two are a 'we' now?

Reece No. It's, um, listen, I'm sorry that's the main thing, I shouldn't have left you alone just cos of some stupid photo but –

Layla It doesn't matter now.

Reece *is awkward, eager. His phone rings.*

Reece   Sorry, I'll just – Hello? Monica? Slow down, what, where?

Layla   Monica?

Reece   Yeah, yeah I'm with Layla now, okay, here –

He gives the phone to **Layla**.

Layla   Monica? Slow down. You're where? In a shed? Why, what? Oh my God, that idiot. Okay, send us your location we'll come get you. Don't panic.

She hands the phone back to **Reece**.

Layla   Monica was locked in a shed by her loving, lovely boyfriend Joe.

Monica   Joe locked me in and I dunno when he's coming back and he's absolutely off his rocker and he thinks me and his mate are getting together so I'm locked in here whilst he is – I dunno, interrogating his mate – you have to just come now.

Layla   She didn't even say sorry, about everything, even though I knew she was, or at least that's what Reece said and I guess this was sort of an emergency.

Monica   Please, this is an emergency and I can't call the police cos my mum can't know I've got a boyfriend!

Layla   Me and Reece go to save her, seems like I'm one of her only friends. We've got a hammer and a spanner and two heartbeats going wild. The padlock isn't even locked properly so we just open it and there she is, Monica with her hair a mess, mascara-stained cheeks and it's pretty obvious she's never been so happy to see me.

Monica   I've never been so happy to see you, babe! And you too, Reece. Thank you so much.

Layla   After the initial celebration of still being alive, it all gets a bit awkward. We go sit at a café as far away from the shed as we can get. We order hot chocolates with extra

cream and marshmallows, even though it's boiling outside
and Monica cries, says she knows Joe is not good for her and
she swears she had a go at him for what he did to me and I
can't speak cos on the one hand I'm glad she's seen the
blinding bright light at last but on the other hand I can't
quite get over how she did me over and stayed with him
even when she found out exactly what he did. Reece
squeezes my hand under the table and it's strange but nice
to feel the skin of someone on mine, it makes me have sparks
inside my stomach and I know he's got a way to go to get
back my full respect, but –

Monica   The thing is, though, it's his birthday tomorrow
and I had all this stuff planned, I don't wanna cancel –

Reece   Monica, he just locked you in a shed –

Monica   Well, it wasn't actually locked though, was it, I just
panicked, and I was a bit flirty with –

Layla   I can't listen to this. Monica. Your boyfriend locked
you up because you spoke to his mate in a way he didn't like.
Hello? He almost ruined my life. I nearly died. Do you know
that? Do you want that to happen to you too?

Monica   I love him.

Layla   That was two weeks ago. She's messaged me to say
she knows I'm right but it's not that easy and she's sorry and
she needs me and I'm like, I'll try. I can try to be there for
her but it's . . . hard. It's a lot to ask . . . considering. I wanna
make this move a new start and I'm not sure Monica can be
someone who comes with me, I just don't know. Reece, well,
maybe I'll see him once a week or so, see how it goes.

For now, I need to worry about tomorrow. Do I go into
school just to do this thing, stand on stage and say what I
want to – or do I just stay silent? Let the past stay where it is
and not have to think about facing a crowd and seeing
somewhere inside it the narrow eyes of Joe and Ryan? Them
muttering threats and names under their hot breath and

making my voice stop, knotted in my throat like a noose that they would never use themselves, they'd just tie it, dangle it, wait for you to stumble into it and then pull. I pull against the feeling in my fists for revenge, I want them to suffer, I want them to feel pain, but then again, I just want to forget and move on. But then even again, I don't want anyone else to go through what I did, I want to rid the world of experiences like that.

She has a moment of pondering. She goes to one of the stacked boxes.

This is my last box to tape up. It's full of all the stuff I didn't want to be without. Laptop, lipglosses, mascara, perfume, headphones, some school stuff that Reece brought for me to catch up on, this book I'm reading, my favourite bra, a photo frame with Kie as a newborn baby and this, a new notepad. It's not packed yet. I haven't written in it. Blank pages.

Maybe I could write my own rules, like Mum said, rules that are written to be helpful to people like me, a new rule book, to share with the school, a rule book to rip up the rules they've got . . . you know what, why not, what have I got to lose? I need a pen!

She is furiously writing.

Two

State of change – **Layla** *is now on stage at school.*

Layla (*spoken word-style statement*)
    I've got some rules to lay down for you today,
    I've got some things I really need to say,
    pay attention for two minutes of your time
    and then rethink the way you live your life.

    Girls are here and we always will be,
    rather than threaten, harass and bully
    think of what could happen if we lived in harmony –
    each of us able to be who we really want to be.

So rule one, consider where you learnt certain things.
Boys in blue, girls in pink,
boys with cars and girls in bows,
we weren't born like this you know.
These things have been created,
differences have been exaggerated,
taken to a place for adverts to make the most of,
making boys think they have to act tough,
making girls think they can never look good enough.
It's made up stuff, you can choose to say, that's enough.

Rule two, forget rules. This is just common sense,
our world would be rubbish without women and men,
both need celebrating, both need remembering
and by the way, to whoever makes up the curriculum,
both need studying!

So now we've done away with a rule book,
we might as well take a good look at ourselves,
sell the version of the future we want to see to our own
brains – I'll tell you what mine would be.
I envision school corridors where names aren't called,
canteens where girls don't feel shy
to eat what they want,
streets where girls don't feel scared
to wear what they want,
classrooms where girls won't be getting touched up,
walks home where we won't have to fight for our clothes,
parties where the boys just know –
if a girl says no, then know that it's no
and if she likes you, she'll tell you so.
If I asked, do you want a tea?
and you said hmm, I dunno, not really,
then I wouldn't make you drink it –
just think on it.
In my future, we all get to live our dreams,
we all get to be paid equally,
we don't have to move schools to escape boys
who think they need to act tough,

we don't need to stand in front of mirrors
wondering when we'll look good enough –
we'll stand in front of each other instead,
friends and loves and sisters and brothers,
it's a future we can make the present,
if we all work on it together.

She walks forward and maybe there's a light directly on her, the others in darkness, and she smiles, she's going to be fine.

End.

Rashida

The Young Vic ran a director's program where emerging directors got to develop and direct a five-minute piece of new writing for a few days, which was then showcased. *Rashida* was written for this and became the first piece of mine that looked at water – something I'd end up sticking with for a while! Emma Roxburgh gave great notes to get this down to a tricky five minutes. It's a difficult timeframe in which to attempt to introduce a character, get a sense of who they are and why, and also give some element of story and place and an ending of sorts.

A non-white woman sits in a sewer, with a rucksack.

Vessels of tunnels
turning this ground below the city into burgeoning burrows.
Layers upon layers of . . . Rats.
Scurrying, hurrying, in their millions apparently.
Shocked at my torchlight in their eyes,
that this small thing could change their direction so
unexpectedly.

Rumbles too. Tubes, trains, lorries delivering perishables
to the people who need what they want
or want what they need
ASAP, no delay.
And water, there's always water.
Dripping, running, trickling,
always forcing its way in.

I was born in a house on a floodplain.
My parents wanted fields.
Coming as they did from sand,
they saw green as a physical marker of their meritocratic rise
to a perceived prominence in a country where, quietly,
they spoke the language
but it was, quite loudly, never their country.
It took my father a while to recognise this.
Once he had – following the helping hand of a few too many
let-downs,
get-downs, 'we don't want you round here's –
he decided that the best way to take a country into one's
heart
was to take a woman of that country into one's arms.

Floodplains aren't named that way for prettiness but for
practicality.
A geological fact in black and white typeset on a map.
Of course, this doesn't put off government-subsidised
developers
whose family trees have a few branches
of low-hanging MPs dangling off them.

No matter how much money gets banked,
the facts in black and white typeset on a map remain.
When it rains heavily over a long period of time,
the plains flood.

One of the times they did, my mum had been alone.
My father by that time had died.
He'd been driving his second wife around to the house of
her parents,
who'd never accept him.
They were arguing, she wrote to me later,
about the levels of humiliation her parents inflicted
by not allowing him past the porch,
letting him watch their family dinner through diamond-
shaped glass.
She didn't think he should be so sensitive,
her father had fought a war for this country, he was stuck in
his ways.
My father reacted with hands that flung words skywards,
leaving the steering wheel to find it's way to a tree
that kept my father's heart finally where it had never
belonged.

The council say my mother never replied
to the severe flood warning phone calls.
Neighbours say the bell went unanswered.
Nobody tried to break in, that would have been rude.
Everyone left and assumed she must have left too.
I'd left long ago, to live with those who spoke English,
a language Mum avoided like phone calls and doorbells
since Dad had left her alone, with sand in her mouth.
She said she could taste it sometimes. Grains of sand,
as if she was in the whirling centre of a storm back home,
skin being pummelled by such tiny particles, usually
harmless,
but when grouped together by wind, blinded and burnt her,
that burning being a salve of sorts.

I went there years ago.
I didn't tell Mum.
I wanted to discover it myself,
without her piles of post-its scribbled with names and addresses
of family members and old school friends
painting my holiday fluorescent with duty.
Nobody knew I was from there.
I was only ever 'the English girl',
my mother's tongue never uncurling from my throat.
I watched a lot. The way they ate, waved, laughed.
I saw a wedding. A funeral.
When loved ones die, they splash water on their lips,
hoping the small drops will carry the songs they sing in grief
to every living thing, so the universe will know what has
been lost.

Only those with a death wish wouldn't have left, they said.
They found her on the ground floor.
The floodwater had gone down by then,
but the watermarks on the wallpaper I was always
embarrassed by
showed that it had bravely attempted to reach the ceiling.
She was bloated, with the waxy skin of a drowned human
whose life has been lost to the very thing
that made them what they were,
the infinitesimal essence of her
flowing through drains, pipes, clouds, sea.

Hers was an unfortunate death, the report said.
The property developers
had provided adequate facilities
for the drainage of surface water;
they couldn't be expected
to provide defences against floodwater.
Who could be defended against a flood?
'They were not responsible for the tragedy.'

I brought her bloated body to London,
a city she had only been to when she stepped off a plane
with a lifetime of expectation.
I wrapped her in a white sheet much later than was right,
it had to be wider than it should have been, her shroud.
I washed her, trailing wet cloths against purple skin,
denting with my touch no matter how softly I sailed over it.
I buried her at a cemetery near where I lived.
I placed flowers there once a month.
I removed the slop of the previous bunch
with my hand in a plastic bag.

I'm comfortable in these damp tunnels of stench
overrun with rats that swim through shit
to get where they're going and, when it rains heavily,
they explode through bloating every now and again.

This water down here,
it's been lived in, used, passed through.
Eventually, it'll run clear again
and the person bathing, drinking, cooking
will have no idea
that I felt it, saw it drip onto the back of a rat
and off again, fearlessly
re-joining the mass,
getting to where it needs to be.

The Power of Plumbing

I worked with Theatre Uncut in Copenhagen, Denmark on a project in 2016, and in 2018 they asked me to contribute a five-minute piece to their 'Power' series. Theatre Uncut's model is brilliant: the pieces are all grouped under a particular issue pertinent to the political moment and are available for free download and performance rights are given the world over for a limited period of time. *The Power of Plumbing* was inspired by reading an article about women in Jordan's workforce being one of the world's lowest and how a growing number of women training to be plumbers, in a country experiencing water crisis and preparing for it to get worse, might change that.

There's not really any directions for this – it is as you wish it to be!

LEAK! Leak! Is there a leak?
Can you see one?
Can you hear it,
the hiss of water wiggling its way out into the world
uncaptured, wasted, wanton?

I won't let that fucking happen.
Let the world know, I stopped the leak.
Let the world know, my fingers found the cracks
and their nimble little tips fucking fixed them.
Superhero with a plunger.
Superhero with temporary plugging gum
and a drum 'n' bass playlist to make me work quicker
than any of these other recruits.
Anybody saving the world needs
a damn good bassline to do it to – trust me.

Mother would not agree,
she needs silence to do what she does,
but what she does is nowhere near as important as what I
do, not anymore.
So she can't moan when the volume goes up now,
I bring the most money back to the house.
We eat off *my* skills, not hers, not Dad's.
How do you like that,
climate change denier teachers?
Those who said I would amount to a pile of flesh
good enough to be married off no later than nineteen,
my decay would set in my twenties,
my features not finessed enough to hold age, apparently.

Well, guess what?
Nobody needs finessed features anymore,
cos what good are they when your eyes are so dry
they have to be covered in near-black lenses
most of the time,
every body looks finessed through that kind of filter.
Ha.

Anyway, in case you haven't guessed
I am one of the blessed ones
who chose to train to become a plumber
and I have power now.
Power in ways it would have been crazy
to imagine before the Water Wars.
Before the greatest commodity became the clear liquid
we used to literally let slip through our fingers
just for the feel of it.

There was a time when a woman would
never be able to bend under a stranger's sink
and say, I can see where the problem is,
it'll take me ten minutes. Pass me the spanner please.
I mean, they physically could of course,
but the very phrase 'pass me the spanner please'
would be interpreted sexually,
because every single thing we did
was interpreted sexually
because every single particle of power
was granted to us on the gravitas of our sexual possibility
by those who may or may not be sexually interested in us
but needed us to know that we were only powerful
if they decided someone, somewhere would be
sexually interested in us eventually.
For example, at nursery, I remember –
one of my first memories actually –
I remember a teacher took a hairclip
to keep my fringe from falling in front of my face –
She said, 'the boys will think you're trying to kiss them
your lovely hair swinging about like that.
And then what would I tell your mummy,
her daughter causing chaos in the nursery!'
She sat me on her lap and laughed
and just like that I knew my hair had the power
to cause chaos in places set up to keep us safe,
to make adults panic and problem solve
and by high school we didn't need to be told

(even though we were of course)
that our skirts were too short,
that we were distracting the teachers,
these men that were paid to teach us
were unable to do their jobs
because of the power our hems held
and we held that high and mighty and proud.
By college I was a bit bored with this sort of power,
it did occur to me, just as things were moving
beyond being environmentally uneasy
to being absolutely fucking terrifying
that entrusting the sum of my power to these men
(who by then I had a bit more . . . knowledge of)
was potentially a life-threatening decision
considering the dire situation we found ourselves in.
I wanted top training in something useful
but usually reserved for boys and I got it –
the unprecedented needs were draining
the gender separation,
they had to take girls on as plumbers
and oh, once they realised we saved more drops per hour
than any boy they'd ever honoured with the
Top Drop Hero Award,
maybe because our fingertips were more sensitive,
maybe because we had to work harder for it,
maybe because our eyes were trained to search for drops
of whatever was being lost from the day we were born –
whatever it was, that was it,
girls were picked out of all the thousands of applicants
to be the senior plumbers,
the new emergency service keeping society surviving –
wait, is that it? The leak?
No, just a dust rat,
damn tails sound like like trickles on these tiles.

Anyway, the Water Wars was alright for some of us,
if you look at it like that.
Which is actually mad,

humankind needing to get to the brink of extinction
before removing (some) gender distinctions
and then only because they had no choice,
not because they were suddenly poised
with some deeper philosophical understanding
of how power being posited in one place,
in one type of person, can never be a power that lasts,
ultimately.
Though can any power at all?
Who knows?
But I know that my ability to get water flowing again
is something I won't be letting go of for a long time.
I'm greedy with the secrets of the service,
I feel like I have always deserved this, to do this, be this.
Even when my little sister asked if I could start
training her up on the basics before her college time comes,
I did feel bad, but I said no, not yet, sis –
this power is fucking mine!
Oh, look, I see it, the leak the leak the leak
should have known, always look up,
a wobbly tear of water about to drop from the ceiling –
CATCH!
Just like that.

This is How it Was

This was originally recorded as an audio piece to be listened to through headphones at a Fuel Theatre installation called *Lock Her Up* at Tate Modern and various other locations, as part of Warwick University's Tate Exchange, *The Production of Truth, Justice and History*.

I wrote *This is How it Was* as a radio game show, after reading research from Warwick University's Rachel Bennett, 'Medical Care, Maternity and Childbirth in Female Prisons, 1850-2000'. It was utterly devastating to learn how maternal care in the present day was completely resonant and hardly improved from 150 years ago. The criminal justice system has been created by men for men and there needs to be a complete overhaul to deal specifically with criminal justice for women. No area is this more starkly obvious than when it comes to maternity and motherhood in prison. For this ten-minute audio piece, I wanted to disorientate the listener but also ground them firmly in the facts of gender inequality being played out within an archaic system that does as little for society as it does for the individual.

Writing in bold is 'radio presenter voice'; all other lines are various characters.

Welcome to today's episode of . . .

'This is how it is
how it was
how it will be'

As always, we will be discussing an issue as it was 'then' and, how it is 'now', and when you hear the (*Ding.*) YOU will be answering 'Then' or 'Now' via text 367821 or hashtagging #ThenNowWinning. And one lucky listener will be winning something we can't say right now exactly what that thing is because it is such an amazing thing we don't want to cause a storming in of the studio but we know you totally know it is worth playing! So fingers on those buttons, people.

Today we look at becoming a mother in prison, that's right, women who have gone into prison pregnant over the ages. Is what we present to you THEN or is it NOW? Remember, now means in the last ten years, then means anything before. Aaaaand today we have ten bonus true or false questions to get you to the top!

We wish you luck, lovely listeners!

is/was/will be/must be/we/you/how/now/then

it it it it it it
is

This is how it is –

Who wants to heavily sentence a mother-to-be?
It's not like I stabbed anyone, I'm no threat to anybody.

TWO YEARS!
Condemned!
We must remember our society
depends on a functioning judicial system,
one whose course must not be perverted,

however sympathetic the motivation may appear to be, this is a system that must NOT be taken for granted.

Ding.

Have we started?

SIGN.

SCAN.

UP.

DOWN.

TURN AROUND, INMATE.

Take those clothes off, put these on, don't take your time.

Crime? What was your crime?

Ding.

Question 1 –

One in three women will lose their home whilst in prison.

True or false?

How will I measure this?
No measuring tape allowed they said, safety risk.
Might try to hang myself with it, they weren't taking the piss.
Said the midwife could do it. Weekly, that is at the hospital, check-ups. But I've been measuring daily. Feeling each millimetre stretch my skin gently, wrapping the tape around and writing it down in my diary. Don't think I'll keep a diary here. Won't want to look back on this,
this is not
I will not
I do not want to look back on –

Ding.

I'm on my back on the table. It's hard it's cold there may be somebody else's bits of body below me I won't know it's too dark to tell they tell me it's fine there's nothing there just the

usual just the womanly woes that brought me here in the
first place so they place me in the cell alone even though I
know there's something there I can feel it moving and I can
feel it beating against the wall of my womb but I have a
womb so I must not know about my own womb and I cannot
point to my own known thoughts I don't have the words and
so I go to my new home and I point at the stars through the
window bars.

Ding.

Question 2 –

**Two hundred and forty-eight children took part in a pilot
visitation scheme at Holloway Prison in 1991, where they
were able to spend the whole day with their mothers. The
children said it made them less worried. The mothers were
happier. However, it was not implemented.**

True or false?

What's an MBU?

Mother and Baby Unit.
Look, just form an orderly queue
to form a face that says, yes,
I am ready to fill in a form –
a form which will inform
everybody about things which will need another form
in order to form a fuller idea
of why you're here, though the form never asks that
the form is shy, it will imply, probe, never be direct,
which is why it needs friends to help
to fill your head, your hands with so many forms
that you don't even know what you're filling out anymore
. . .
forms are the formal way we operate our best practice to
keep you all in tip-top form during 'your stay' here (a form
will never say 'your incarceration')
even though a stay here is not what the human mind, body,
soul was formed for, our feedback forms will help you tell us

how we can form a more conducive environment to inform your speedy recovery/reintegration/reform
REFORM
REFORM
Form an orderly queue, please.

Ding.

What's an MBU?

Mother and Baby Unit.
Limited places. And you know, there's been a lot of cuts, so the rooms might be there, but not enough staff to make sure it's safe.

Ding.

Question 3 –

Three per cent of women prisoners are assessed as being a serious risk to the public. Therefore, 97 per cent of women prisoners are *not* a serious risk to the public.

True or false?

Do you think Mother and Baby Units are a way of making motherhood a method of reform?

I actually believe in the potential remedial effects of having babies in the prison – not just for their own mothers but also for other women in the prison. The advantages to the mother of their presence in the prison are obvious; and into the cold existence of other women too, the children bring a touch of something human. The crowing of a baby breaks the silence and to many women the mere sight of a child is a relief.

Ding.

Question 4 –

Forty per cent of women prisoners have received mental health treatment in the year before coming to prison.

Almost the same amount have attempted suicide at some point in their lives.

True or false?

Question 5 –

Five per cent of the UK prison population is women. Yet they account for a third of all self-harm incidents.

True or false?

Question 6 –

Sixty-six per cent of women in prison have dependent children, almost half are under five years old.

True or –

The doctor's word was false. There was something in there. It was a girl. She was the one banging on my womb wall, the womb wall I was told I didn't know enough about to know there was something soon to come out. She came out. The floor was harder than that table was where he told me the false words and so her head hurt, her little head was very hurt and now she's the third star I can see out of the bars, just there. I wait all day for a cloudless night so I can stare at her.

Ding.

Question 7 –

Seven per cent more likely to reoffend are women who are given prison sentences rather than community service orders.

True or false?

We're running out of time now so –

Eight –

Eighty-five is the percentage increase of women in prison over the last ten years.

True or false?

Nine –

Nine years on the job and a senior official says men always have someone waiting at the gates, women are 90 per cent likely to walk out alone.

True or true or are they all true it says they are all –

Ten –

Ten out of twenty women in prison report having suffered sexual abuse during childhood.

True or –

I was born in a ward full to the brim,
no private room,
no space for my mum to breathe deeply.
My mum was silent, when she had me.
Went through all that searing propulsion
all those parachuting pain bombs
without so much as a
aaaaaaaah
certainly no
fuuuuuucccckkk thissss!
She's very proud of that, my mum.

I screamed and screamed when my little one
scraped her way along my insides.
I screamed for drugs, but it was too far along.
I screamed for me, face pushed into a gas and air mask,
Without my mum to disapprove of my vocal display, without
a real friend to lay cool cloths on my head.
And I screamed for her, my baby, of course I did.
For her to be born to a criminal mother,
a lying, criminal mother who'd be forced to give her away
cos there was no space here no space no staff no resources
away from her own arms to another,
to someone
who never felt the first fizz of her little heart,

who never told her stories before she could hear,
who never swayed with the rhythm of her kicks
and I screamed after I screamed at them all –
This can't be right, this little human here, here in my arms
that are made of the same flesh as hers, right, these arms
holding this baby, my flesh, well, she cries and when she
does, do you know what happens? My boobs leak, my
fucking boobs leak when my newborn daughter cries,
because that's how it works, that is how it works –
Who is gonna have dripping nipples when she cries, when
her little eyes close up and she wails her lungs away are your
breasts gonna swell to say I'm ready, I have what you want
my little angel I'm here, I'm here, I'm here, I'm here I'm
here I'm here
I will always be here
for you
because I am your mother
even if I did do wrong
even if I did speed along a country lane
one stupid time
nobody can ever really
take you away from me.
I am here.

Ding. Ding. Ding.

9 781350 143555